MW00946619

The *Adorning* of a WOMAN

SCHONSHARY CHIFFON

All biblical scriptures written according to the Authorized King James version of the Holy Bible.

WestBow Press books may be ordered through booksellers or by contacting:

WestBow Press
A Division of Thomas Nelson
1663 Liberty Drive
Bloomington, IN 47403
www.westbowpress.com
1-(866) 928-1240

ISBN: 978-1-4497-4420-5 (e)
ISBN: 978-1-4497-4421-2 (sc)
ISBN: 978-1-4497-4422-9 (hc)

Library of Congress Control Number: 2012905342

Printed in the United States of America

WestBow Press rev. date: 06/12/2012

DEDICATION

This book is dedicated to everyone who supported and believed in my vision. I *love* and *appreciate* each of you.

READERS:

This book has been simply written so that a child could grasp the information inside and not err.

And an highway shall be there, and a way, and it shall be called The way of holiness; the unclean shall not pass over it; but it shall be for those: the wayfaring men, though fools, shall not err therein (Isaiah 35:8).

INTRODUCTION

Most women dedicate the majority of their time focusing on their outer appearance, and we diet like crazy while spending countless hours in the gym. We pay more attention to hairstyles and fashion than anything else. Sadly, most women spend more time in the mirror admiring their beauty than in the presence of the Almighty God! There isn't anything wrong with being beautiful, but remember that the true beauty of a woman lies within her heart, and not in her flesh or the things she adorns herself with. (1 Samuel 16:7)

> But the LORD said unto Samuel, Look not on his countenance or on the height of his stature; because I have refused him: for the LORD seeth not as man seeth; for man looketh on the outward appearance, but the LORD looketh on the heart.
>
> As in water face answereth to face, so the heart of man to man (Proverbs 27:19)

Happy is the man that feareth alway: but he that hardeneth his heart shall fall into mischief (Proverbs 28:14).

O generation of vipers, how can ye, being evil, speak good things? For out of the abundance of the heart the mouth speaketh (Matthew 12:34).

For this people's heart is waxed gross, and their ears are dull of hearing, and their eyes they have closed; lest at any time they should see with their eyes, and hear with their ears, and should understand with their heart, and should be converted, and I should heal them (Matthew 13:15).

But those things which proceed out of the mouth come forth from the heart; and they defile the man (Matthew 15:18).

A good man out of the good treasure of his heart bringeth forth that which is good; and an evil man out of the evil treasure of his heart bringeth forth that which is evil: for of the abundance of the heart his mouth speaketh (Luke 6:45).

I believe that women were born to be servants of the almighty God. In fact, women are more submissive to the Word of God than most men. The next time you're attending church services, take a minute to count the ratio between all of the men and women who are present. I'm certain that you will agree with me. It is my belief that because of the obedience of women to the Word of God, he has used us as vessels since the beginning of time. Therefore, we must return to our rightful place in God.

> And Ruth said, intreat me not to leave thee, or return from following after thee: for wither thou goest, I will go; and where thou lodgest, I will lodge: thy people shall be my people, and thou GOD my GOD (Ruth 1:16).

And Deb'-o-rah a prophetess, the wife of Lap'-i-doth, she judged Israel at that time (Judges 4:4).

And she answered and said unto him, Yes, LORD: yet the dogs under the table eat of the children's crumbs. And he said unto her, For this saying go thy way; the devil is gone out of thy daughter (Mark 7:28-29).

And certain women, which had been healed of evil spirits and infirmities, Mary called Mag-da-le'-ne, out of whom went seven devils (Luke 8:2)

And Jo-an'-na the wife of Chu'-za Herod's steward, and Susanna, and many others, which ministered unto him of their substance (Luke 8:3)

And, behold, a woman in the city, which was sinner, when she knew that Jesus sat at meat in the Pharisee's house, brought an alabaster box of ointment, (Luke 7:37)

And stood at his feet behind him weeping, and began to wash his feet with tears, and did wipe them with the hairs of her head, and kissed his feet, and anointed them with the ointment. (Luke 7:38)

And he turned to the woman, and said unto Simon, Seest thou this woman? I entered into thine house, thou gavest me no water for my feet: but she hath washed my feet with tears, and wiped them with the hairs of her head. (Luke 7:44)

Thou gavest me no kiss: but this woman since the time I came in hath not ceased to kiss my feet. (Luke 7:45)

My head with oil thou didst not anoint: but this woman hath anointed my feet with ointment. (Luke 7:46)

And the angel answered and said unto the women, Fear not ye: for I know that ye seek JESUS, which was crucified. He is not here: for he is risen, as he said. Come, see the place where the LORD lay. And go quickly, and tell his disciples that he is risen from the dead; and, behold, he goeth before you into Galilee; there shall ye see him: lo, I have told you. And they departed quickly from the selpulchere with fear and great joy; and did run to bring his disciples word (Matthew 28:5-8).

When I call to remembrance the unfeigned faith that is in thee, which dwelt first in thy grandmother LO'-is, and thy mother Eu-ni'-ce; and I am persuaded that in thee also (2 Timothy 1:5).

CHAPTER ONE

OBEDIENCE

Obedience to the Word of God is what determines our fate. By obeying the will of God, we're able to receive his gift of inheritance. There are two vital components in serving God: obedience and love. We were instructed to obey God and love him with all of our hearts, souls, and might.

And thou shalt love the LORD thy GOD with all thine heart, and with all thy soul, and with all thy might (Deuteronomy 6:5).

Obeying the Word of God in all matters is what prevents curses from entering your home and allows you to maintain your relationship with almighty God. Believe it or not, obeying the Word of God will aid you in maintaining fruitful relationships with others. However, it is through your disobedience to the Word of God that the enemy is able to gain entry into your life to destroy it. You must be extremely cautious in your decision-making, speaking, and actions. Women, God has given us specific instructions on how to conduct ourselves, especially in marriage. As we journey through each chapter, let's all adorn ourselves in the true Word of God.

How then shall they call on him in whom they have not believed? and how shall they believe in him of whom they have not heard? and how shall they hear without a preacher? (Romans 10:14)

Most people ignore both God and his Word until storms start raging in their lives, and once the storms start, they become instant Christians. I used the word "instant" only to express how quickly some folks become religious. Then, of course, after Jesus has rebuked the wind and rain in their lives, they return to their old ways. I advise you that whatever you do in Jesus's name, let it be *real,* because whenever you need the help of God, you want to be able to call on his name with confidence that he'll be there. You don't want to doubt that God will rescue you because of your disobedience.

When you are *obedient* to God, you may seek him with expectancy. God then gives you the authority to speak life into your circumstances and the power to rebuke Satan. But how can you rebuke Satan if you have been serving him all day? Remember, your obedience to God enables him to give you Holy Ghost's power, and it's through your disobedience that you lose that very same power. You don't have to be a thief, murderer, or adulterer to disobey the Word of God. You may be a faithful church member, a faithful wife, a good mother, a tither, a prayer warrior, and the preacher's wife. You may have love for all of humanity, compassion, and charity, but if you aren't submissive to your husband, then you are disobedient to the Word of God. As a result of your behavior, your prayers *will be hindered because God will never bless a home in rebellion.*

In today's society, where most women are independent and self-reliant, submission appears to be a thing of the past. Satan has deceived more women into believing that they are equal to men than ever before (refer to 1 Peter 3:7 below). Some women are fooled into believing that because their income is greater than their spouses', those men don't deserve their respect. Other women feel that because they possess a higher level of education than their spouses, their husbands are incapable of making good decisions. Therefore, more women are wearing the pants in their home than men, and this is definitely outside of the will of God!

I'm concerned as to how a woman expects her husband to hold her gently during the night when she's so very mannish during the day. I've learned through experience that a man hates it when his wife is defiant. When you refuse to *obey* your husband, you bring division between the two of you. Don't get any misconceptions: I'm not saying you don't have a voice. Yes, it is all right to disagree with your husband, but it is not all right to disagree upon all things. However, *godly* wisdom teaches you when to stand firm or when to kneel and pray about certain matters while leaving them in the hands of the almighty God. All women must learn to trust in God no matter how difficult their problems appear to be. Trusting God is an act of *obedience* to his Word.

Likewise, ye husbands, dwell with them according to knowledge, giving honour unto the wife, as unto the weaker vessel, and as being heirs together of the grace of life; that your prayers be not hindered (1 Peter 3:7).

In those days was Hez-e-ki'-ah sick unto death. And Isaiah the prophet the son of Amoz came unto him, and said unto him, Thus saith the LORD, Set thine house in order: for thou shalt die and not live (Isaiah 38:1).

TRUST in the LORD with all thine heart; and lean not unto thine own understanding (Proverbs 3:5).

Trust in the LORD, and do good; so shalt thou dwell in the land, and verily thou shalt be fed (Psalm 37:3).

Commit thy way unto the LORD; trust also in him; and he shall bring it to pass (Psalm 37:5).

So shall I have wherewith to answer him that reproacheth me: for I trust in thy word (Psalm 119:42).

Blessed is the man that trusteth in the LORD, and whose hope the LORD is (Jeremiah 17:7).

And they that know thy name will put their trust in thee: for thou, LORD, hast not forsaken them that seek thee (Psalm 9:10).

Trust ye in the LORD for ever: for in the LORD JE-HO'-VAH is everlasting strength (Isaiah 26:4).

Who is among you that feareth the LORD, that obeyeth the voice of his servant, that walketh in darkness, and hath no light? let him trust in the name of the LORD, and stay upon his God (Isaiah 50:10).

He that handleth a matter wisely shall find good: and whoso trusteth in the LORD, happy is he (Proverbs 16:20).

Offer the sacrifices of righteousness, and put your trust in the LORD (Psalm 4:5).

Then Peter and other apostles answered and said, We ought to OBEY GOD rather than man (Acts 5:29).

WHAT ARE CURSES?

According to Webster's New Compact Dictionary, a curse is a prayer or wish for harm to come to someone or something. Have you ever seen a family in which the majority of its members are alcoholics, or have you ever noticed a family in which everyone suffered from mental disorders? These are usually signs of a curse. Unfortunately, there are many people who are living under a curse that was started by the sins of their forefathers. Some signs of a curse are a continual negative pattern of a trait passed down from generation to generation or anything that seems to be a constant battle or problem.

HOW ARE CURSES STARTED?

Curses start when we decide to disobey the Word of God. The enemy uses disobedience to gain entry into our lives to destroy us.

WHAT IS DISOBEDIENCE?

According to Webster's New Compact Dictionary, disobedience is the act of refusing to obey or failing to obey. Adam and Eve's decision to eat of the forbidden fruit is a primary example of the act of disobedience. As a result of their disobedience, all humanity still lives under a curse. To this very day, women suffer the pain of childbirth, men are forced to work all the days of their lives, people die, the serpent crawls upon his belly, and enmity is present between him (the serpent) and the woman and her offspring.

Shortly after eating the forbidden fruit, the quality of life for both Adam and Eve was instantly changed. They no longer enjoyed the comfort the Lord had provided them in the Garden of Eden. They were driven out of the garden, and their sources of food were reduced, so they were forced to work so they could eat. Sin separates humanity from God, and in addition, it starts curses in our lives. As a result of Adam and Eve's disobedience to the Word of God, much evil befell them. One evil in particular was that their son, Cain, murdered his brother, Abel.

CAN CURSES BE BROKEN?

Curses can be broken through sincere repentance, forsaking your sins, and exercising your spiritual authority, and accompanying these things by fervent *prayer.*

And when the woman saw that the tree was good for food, and that it was pleasant to the eyes, and a tree to be desired to make one wise, she took of the fruit thereof, and did eat, and gave also unto her husband with her; and he did eat (Genesis 3:6).

Unto the woman he said, I will greatly multiply thy sorrow and thy conception, in sorrow thou shalt bring forth children; and thy desire shall be to thy husband, and he shall rule over thee (Genesis 3:16).

And unto Adam he said, Because thou hast hearkened unto the voice of thy wife, and hast eaten of the tree, of which I commanded thee, saying, Thou shalt not eat of it: cursed is the ground for thy sake; in sorrow shalt thou eat of it all the days of thy life (Genesis 3:17).

Thorns also and thistles shall it bring forth to thee; and thou shalt eat the herb of the field. In the sweat of thy face shalt thy eat bread, till thou return unto the ground; for out of it was thou taken: for dust thou art, and unto dust shalt thou return (Genesis 3:18-19).

And Cain talked with Abel his brother: and it came to pass, when they were in the field, that Cain rose up against Abel his brother, and slew him (Genesis 4:8).

And it came to pass, that at midnight the LORD smote all the firstborn in the land of Egypt, from the firstborn of Pharaoh that sat on his throne unto the firstborn of the captive that was in the dungeon;

and all the firstborn of cattle. And Pharaoh rose up in the night, he, and all his servants, and all the Egyptians; and there was a great cry in Egypt; for there was not a house where there was not one dead (Exodus 12:29-30).

And Samuel said, Hath the LORD as great delight in burnt offerings and sacrifices, as in obeying the voice of the LORD? Behold, to obey is better than sacrifice, and to hearken than the fat of rams (1 Samuel 15:22).

And a curse, if ye will not obey the commandments of the LORD your God, but turn aside out of the way which I command you this day, to go after other gods, which ye have not known (Deuteronomy 11:28).

But if ye will not obey the voice of the LORD, but rebel against the commandment of the LORD, then shall the hand of the LORD be against you, as it was against your fathers (1 Samuel 12:15).

For the children of Israel walked forty years in the wilderness, till all the people that were men of war, which came out of Egypt, were consumed, because they obeyed not the voice of the LORD: unto whom the LORD sware that he would not show them the land, which the LORD sware unto their fathers that he would give us, a land that floweth with milk and honey (Joshua 5:6).

If it do evil in my sight, that it obey not my voice, then I will repent of the good, wherewith I said I would benefit them (Jeremiah 18:10).

But if they will not obey, I will utterly pluck up and destroy that nation, saith the LORD (Jeremiah 12:17).

And the LORD saith, Because they have forsaken my law which I set before them, and have not obeyed my voice, neither walked therein... But have walked after the imagination of their own heart and after Ba'-a-lim, which their fathers taught them Therefore thus saith the LORD OF HOSTS, THE God of Israel; Behold, I will feed them, even this people, with wormwood, and give them water of gall to drink (Jeremiah 9:13,14,15).

And Na'-dab and A-bi'-hu, the sons of Aaron, took either of them his censer, and put fire therein, and put incense thereon, and offered strange fire before the LORD, which he commanded them not (Leviticus 10:1).

And Pharaoh said, Who is the LORD, that I should obey his voice to let Israel go? I know not the LORD, neither will I let Israel go (Exodus 5:2).

Yet I had planted thee a noble vine, wholly a right seed: how then art thou turned into the degenerate plant of a strange vine unto me? (Jeremiah 2:21)

I have sent also unto you all my servants the prophets, rising up early and sending them, saying, Return ye now every man from his evil way, and amend your doings, and go not after other gods to serve them, and ye shall dwell in the land which I have given to you and to your fathers: but ye have not inclined your ear, nor hearkened unto me (Jeremiah 35:15).

They kept not the covenant of God, and refused to walk in his law . . . How oft did they provoke him in the wilderness, and grieve him in the desert! (Psalm 78:10, 40).

Thou shalt not bow down thyself to them, nor serve them: for I the LORD thy God am a jealous God, visiting the iniquity of the fathers upon the children unto the third and fourth generation of them that hate me (Exodus 20:5).

Sanctify yourselves therefore, and be ye holy: for I am the LORD your God (Leviticus 20:7).

In that I command thee this day to love the LORD thy God, to walk in his ways, and to keep his commandments and his statues and his judgments, that thou mayest live and multiply: and the LORD thy God shall bless thee in the land whether thou goest to possess it (Deuteronomy 30:16).

And in thy seed shall all the nations of the earth be blessed; because thou hast obeyed my voice (Genesis 22:18).

Thus did Noah; according to all that God commanded him, so did he (Genesis 6:22).

And he took the book of the covenant, and read in the audience of the people: and they said, All that the LORD hath said will we do, and be obedient (Exodus 24:7).

If ye love me, keep my commandments (John 14:15).

And being found in fashion as a man, he humbled himself, and became obedient unto death, even the death of the cross (Philippians 2:8).

As obedient children, not fashioning yourselves according to the former lusts in your ignorance: (1 Peter 1:14).

For as by one man's disobedience many were made sinners, so by the obedience of one shall many be made righteous (Romans 5:19).

For he shall give his angels charge over thee, to keep thee in all thy ways (Psalm 91:11).

Chapter Two

MARRIAGE

And the rib, which the LORD God had taken from man, made he a woman, and brought her unto man. And Adam said, This is now bone of my bones, and flesh of my flesh: she shall be called Woman, because she was taken out of Man (Genesis 2:22-23).

Marriage is a binding contract between a male and female that is ordained by God. It is a vow that a man and woman commit unto God which is not revocable.

When thou vowest a vow unto God, defer not to pay it; for he hath no pleasure in fools: pay that which thou hast vowed. Better is it that thou shouldest not vow, than that thou shouldest vow and not pay (Ecclesiastes 5:4-5).

Prior to marriage, one must be certain that he or she is mentally prepared to accept the responsibilities of what marriage entails. Marriage consists of love, longsuffering, commitment, communication, dedication, faithfulness, patience, and giving.

Nevertheless, to avoid fornication, let every man have his own wife, and let every woman have her own husband (1 Corinthians 7:2). However, in today's society, the concept of marriage has been misconstrued, and married couples are forsaking their wedding vows as well as the ordinances of God. They are failing to practice monogamy, increasing the divorce rate.

The Pharisees also came unto him, tempting him, and saying unto him, Is it lawful for a man to put away his wife for every cause? And he answered and said unto them, Have ye not read, that he which made them at the beginning made them male and female. And said for this cause shall a man leave father and mother, and shall cleave to his wife: and they twain shall be one flesh? Wherefore they are no more twain, but one flesh. What therefore God has joined together, let not man put asunder (Matthew 19:3-6).

According to the Bible, from the beginning, divorce was not so.

They say unto him, Why did Moses then command to give a writing of divorcement, and to put her away? He saith unto them, Moses because of the hardness of your hearts suffered you to put away your wives: but from the beginning it was not so (Matthew 19:7-8).

The wife is bound by the law as long as her husband liveth; but if her husband be dead, she is at liberty to be married to whom she will; only in the Lord (1 Corinthians 7:39).

God allowed divorce under specific circumstances.

And I say unto you, Whosoever shall put away his wife, except it be for fornication, and shall marry another, committeth adultery: and whoso marrieth her which is put away doth commit adultery (Matthew 19:9).

In conclusion, the implementation of the ordinances of God will assist you in maximizing your efforts to obtain a fruitful marriage.

A good man is definitely difficult to find—especially nowadays, when more men are lovers of themselves than they are of God. Allow me to share my definition of a good man. Since times are much different than they were when I was growing up, your definition of a good man may differ from mine.

A good man isn't a perfect man but one who is a provider for his household. Although he may not be wealthy, he evades excuses and does what is necessary to provide for his family. Even when he's out of work, he will seek diligently—daily—until he finds employment. If he can't find a job that meets his standards, he'll settle for a job that is beneath his standards in order to bring a paycheck home to his family. He will work underpaid while he continues to seek a job of higher income. This is a man who deserves your respect, and you shouldn't have any problems respecting him.

I realize that sometimes when you're experiencing difficulties in your marriage or finances, the idea of an extramarital affair appears to be an interesting way to escape reality. Why would you commit adultery when it isn't going to solve the problem? In fact, it will only complicate the problem. When someone makes the decision to cheat, he or she must understand the dangers of it.

First of all, your health is at risk, and everything that you've worked so hard to build is in jeopardy. For example, your home, finances, and marriage are all in jeopardy. When you decide to cheat, you must be aware of the consequences and the domino effect that they have. Therefore, when you are experiencing problems in your marriage, just *pray* for the strength to endure. In fact, a God-fearing woman would never defile her body by sleeping with two men, because she knows that God has created her both beautiful and unique. And although she is experiencing marital problems, she doesn't need another man to define who she is. Therefore, she will never lower her standards.

A God-fearing woman possesses an inner strength that keeps her from falling for any man outside of her husband. She has a *fear* of God which keeps her faithful to her husband, no matter what problems she encounters in her marriage. No matter how deep or difficult her problems may be or how often they occur, in the midst of her storm, she holds steadfast to God's Word, praying, fasting, and singing spiritual hymns that will help to strengthen her along the way. As she reaches for the hem of God's garment, she trusts the almighty God with expectancy to bring her through! No man—including her husband—can take the place of the almighty God in her life!

Who shall separate us from the love of Christ? Shall tribulation, or distress, or persecution, or famine, or nakedness, or peril, or sword? . . . For I am persuaded, that neither death, nor life, nor angels, nor principalities, nor powers, nor things present, nor things to come, Nor height, nor depth, nor any other creature, shall be able to separate us from the love of God, which is in Christ Jesus our Lord (Romans 8:35,38-39).

Now unto him that is able to do exceeding abundantly above all that we ask or think, according to the power that worketh in us (Ephesians 3:20).

Strength and honour are her clothing; and she shall rejoice in time to come (Proverbs 31:25).

Let the husband render unto the wife due benevolence: and likewise also the wife unto the husband (1 Corinthians 7:3).

HONORING YOUR HUSBAND

You must never dishonor your husband—especially in the presence of others or your children. Some men are authority figures who are always in the public eye. Therefore, you must know how to govern yourself accordingly at all times. Honoring your husband is one of the essential ingredients to a successful marriage. Also, when accompanying your husband to an engagement, you should dress age-appropriately, smile, and greet other attending guests. Don't attempt to make yourself known to others without being introduced just because you may feel that your husband is taking longer than you anticipated introducing who you are.

If your husband requires you to do something that you disagree with or you simply aren't feeling up to, do it as long as it isn't contrary to the Word of God. If you have any concerns about anything, speak to him in private concerning the matter. Remember, you want your husband to be proud to have you as a wife even in years to come. Never rebel against your husband in the presence of others. Again, if there is a problem concerning a matter, you must consider addressing the issue when the two of you are alone. When you are in the company of other people, you must always remember that someone is observing your behavior toward your husband.

A wife is supposed to lead the younger women by example, and your positive behavior will teach them how to behave toward their husbands. But if you dishonor your husband, you cannot possibly teach another woman anything effectively. In fact, what husband would allow his wife to keep company with a woman who disrespects her husband?

Don't rebel against your husband as long as what he says isn't contrary to the Word of God. The spirit of rebellion is responsible for countless divorces. If you have a problem with honoring your husband, *pray* that God changes your heart. If you neglect to change your ways, the enemy is setting you up for a letdown. You must reject the spirit of rebellion, as it is responsible for many divorces as well as the loss of Queen Vash'-ti's royal estate that was given to another who was better than she, Queen Esther.

On the seventh day, when the heart of the king was merry with wine, he commanded Me-hu'-man, Biz'-tha, Har-bo'-na, Big'-tha, and A-bag'-tha, Ze'-thar, and Car'-cas, the seven chamberlains that served in the presence of A-has-u-e'-rus the king, To bring Vash'-ti the queen before the king with the crown royal, to shew the people and the princes her beauty: for she was fair to look on. But the queen Vash'-ti refused to come at the king's commandment by his chamberlains: therefore was the king very wroth, and his anger burned in him. Then the king said to the wise men, which knew the times, (for so was the king's manner toward all that knew law and judgment: And the next unto him was Car-she'-na, She'-thar, Ad-ma'-tha, Tar'-shish, Me'-res, Mar'-se-na, and Me-mu'-can, the seven princes of Persia and Me'-dia, which saw the king's face, and which sat the first in the kingdom;) What shall we do unto the queen Vash'-ti according to the law, because she hath not performed the commandment of the king A-has-u-e'-rus by the chamberlains? And Me-mu'-can answered before the king and the princes, Vash'-ti the queen hath not done wrong to the king only, but also to all the princes, and to all the people that are in all the provinces of the king A-has-u-e'-rus. For this deed of the queen shall come abroad unto all women, so that they shall despise their husbands in their eyes, when it shall be reported, The king A-has-u-e'-rus commanded Vash'-ti the queen to be brought in before him, but she came not. Likewise shall the ladies of Persia and Me'-di-a say this day unto all the king's princes, which have heard of the deed of the queen. Thus shall there arise too much contempt and wrath. If it please the king, let there go a royal commandment from him, and let it be written among the laws of the Persians and the Medes, that it be not altered, That Vash'-ti come no more before king A-has-u-e'-rus; and let the king give her royal estate unto another that is better than she. And when the king's decree which he shall make shall be published throughout all his empire, (for it is great,) all the wives shall give to their husbands honour, both to great and small, And the saying pleased the king and the princes; and the king did according to the word of Me-mu'-can. (Ester 1:10-21).

In conclusion, most women have a bad habit of interrupting their husbands while they are engaging in a conversation with others. Some women are oblivious of their actions while other women intentionally embarrass their husbands in the presence of others. In an effort to respect your husband, you should avoid interrupting his conversation in attempt to correct, remind, or agree with him unless he asks you otherwise.

Your behavior toward your husband will display the level of respect that you have for him. Also, it will teach the younger women how to conduct themselves as wives. Trust in me; you don't have to always speak, because you can learn much more by listening than you will by speaking!

Let the women learn in silence with all subjection (1 Timothy 2:11).

RESPONSIBILITIES OF A WIFE

Marriage is honourable in all, and the bed undefiled: but whoremongers and adulterers GOD will judge (Hebrews 13:4).

Often women complain that their husbands' sex drives are too high. I strongly suggest that you *pray* that God increases your sex drive if you are experiencing this problem, because the both of you need to be of the same accord in order for the marriage to work. All wives must be extremely cautious not to fail in being attentive to the needs of their husbands.

I know that life can get stressful—especially since a woman's work is always incomplete—but no matter how rough your day has been or how tired you are, ask God for the strength to please your husband sexually. Even if you have to roll over on top him and just lie there while he does the job alone, I'm certain that your husband will give you credit for trying.

You must express your love and passion for your husband as often as possible. It is important that you never allow several days, weeks, or months to pass without making love to him unless legitimate reasons prohibit it, and *always* ensure that you thoroughly explain the situation to him.

And God blessed them, and God said unto them, Be fruitful and multiply, and replenish the earth, and subdue it: and have dominion over the fish of the sea, and over the fowl of the air, and over every living thing that moveth upon the earth (Genesis 1:28).

Defraud ye not one the other, except it be with consent for a time, that ye may give yourselves to fasting and prayer; and come together again, that Satan tempt you not for your incontinency (1 Corinthians 7:5).

Let him kiss me with the kisses of his mouth: for thy love is better than wine. A bundle of myrrh is my wellbeloved unto me; he shall lie all night betwixt my breasts (Song of Solomon 1:2, 13).

His left hand is under my head, and his right hand doth embrace me. My beloved is like a roe or a young hart: behold, he standeth behind our wall, he looketh forth at the windows, shewing himself through the lattice. My beloved spake, and said unto me, Rise up, my love, my fair one, and come away. (Song of Solomon 2:6, 9-10).

Thy lips, O my spouse, drop as the honeycomb: honey and milk are under thy tongue; and the smell of thy garments is like the smell of Leb'anon (Song of Solomon 4:11).

All wives must be aware that neglecting the needs of their husbands only opens the door for the enemy to present the men to other women. In today's society, most woman lack morals, values, and self-esteem. Therefore, they can care less that men are married. These women will perform sexual acts on married men that their wives will have to be born again (through natural birth) to learn, and if the husbands didn't know the difference, the husbands would confuse the other women with their wives. I advise all wives to be wise and take care of the needs of their own husbands; this could prevent any potential problems that may involve other women.

The wife hath not power of her own body, but the husband: and likewise also the husband hath not power of his own body, but the wife. (1 Corinthians 7:4).

Submitting yourselves one to another in the fear of God. Wives, submit yourselves unto your own husbands, as unto the Lord. For the husband is the head of the wife, even as Christ is the head of the church: and he is the savior of the body. Therefore as the church is subject unto Christ, so let the wives be to their own husbands in every thing. Husbands love your wives, even as Christ also loved the church, and gave himself for it. That he might sanctify and cleanse it with the washing of the water by the word. That he might present it to himself a glorious church, not having spot, or wrinkle, or any such thing; but that it should be holy and without blemish. So ought men to love their wives as their own bodies. He that loveth his wife loveth himself. For no man ever yet hateth his own flesh; but nourisheth and cherisheth it, even as the Lord the church: For we are members of his body, of his flesh, and of his bones. For this cause shall a man leave his father and mother, and shall be joined unto his wife, and they two shall be one flesh (Ephesians 5:21-31).

Always dress appealing for your husband, although not in a revealing way in public. In fact, you should always practice dressing modestly in public. However, there aren't any limitations on what you can or cannot wear in your bedroom. In the privacy of your bedroom, you may wear sexy lingerie, thongs, booty shorts, or simply nothing at all! You always want to appear sexy to your husband, as sexiness plays a major role in his attractiveness to you. You can't expect him to become aroused if you get into bed dressed like a nun.

Some women are sexy but are unsure of how to work their husbands in bed. If that is the case, I advise you to ask him to teach you. I know that this all sounds a bit extreme, but you must put forth the maximum effort in maintaining an interesting sex life—and what better person is there to ask than him? After all, he knows how he wants to be pleased.

Please don't ask another woman (girlfriend) how to please your husband, because you may later discover that she's sleeping with him. Also, if you've been married for more than five years, you must really strive to maintain a level of spice in your bedroom. Always remember that time doesn't maintain a healthy marriage or prevent a divorce. A healthy marriage requires the maximum effort from both husband and wife to maintain. In fact, marriage requires more effort to keep your husband than was required when you were dating him.

You can't go to hell for pleasing your husband in bed as long as it's your husband and not someone else's. Also, the bed is undefiled to a married *couple.* Therefore, there shouldn't be a third person invited into your bed except the Holy Ghost! God doesn't require you to do anything pleasing to your husband that is contrary to his Word.

Marriage is honourable in all, and the bed undefiled: but whoremongers and adulterers God will judge (Hebrews 13:4).

MEAL PREPARATION

It seems that cooking has become a thing of the past, and eating out has become a monthly bill in most homes. The older women prepared meals for their families daily. In fact, my mother was dedicated to preparing home-cooked meals, so my siblings and I barely ate fast food while growing up. Whenever we were fortunate to eat fast food, we didn't take it for granted, because we understood that we wouldn't get that privilege again for a long time.

It's important to prepare home-cooked meals, as the route to a man's heart begins at his stomach. If you aren't a great cook, you can gather recipes from older women or purchase a good cookbook. I believe that your husband will appreciate your efforts to please him even if the food isn't so great in the beginning. Try to prepare home-cooked meals more often to eliminate the costs of dining out; your husband will appreciate that, too.

A wise woman also ensures that her family eats healthy meals each day. If you are aware that your schedule will be hectic on a particular day, then you should prepare your meal the day prior. This will ensure that your family will receive a nice, home-cooked meal. You can't eliminate cooking and then expect your husband to recognize you as a great wife. Prepare home-cooked meals as often as possible.

In addition, it is wise to *pray* prior to preparing each meal and then prepare your meals with love and joy. When your husband tastes the food, he will taste the love you have poured inside! If possible, put forth more effort in preparing Sunday dinners. Believe me; your family will begin looking forward to the quality time you all will spend together at the dinner table.

She is like the merchants' ships; she bringeth her food from afar. She riseth also while it is yet night, and giveth meat to her household, and a portion to her maidens (Proverbs 31:14-15).

HOUSEKEEPING

Every woman must maintain a clean home and clean laundry. After a long, hard day of work, your husband would like to come home to a clean home along with a nice, hot, cooked meal. He doesn't want to come to wash dishes so that you can prepare his meals, as this should be done prior to his arrival. The bedroom should be clean and the bed nice and cozy, with clean linens. Your husband shouldn't have to do the laundry before he can put clean linens on the bed.

Your home should always smell good. In fact, it's great to keep scented candles and nice fragrances in the home. The bathroom must be clean as well. You can also take it a step further by placing your husband's bath towels, underwear, and pajamas in the bathroom prior to his arrival. Your daughters will observe your behavior, and when they come of age and are married, they will know how to treat their husbands—after all, children pattern after what they observe. Your behavior will display to your husband the love and appreciation that you have for his support of the family.

Women will be absolutely amazed how simple things such as these could make big differences in their marriage. All your husband really wants is to be loved, respected, and appreciated. Isn't that simple?

The aged women likewise, that they be in behaviour as becometh holiness, not false accusers, not given to much wine, teachers of good things; That they may teach the young women to be sober, to love their husbands, to love their children, To be discreet, chaste, keepers at home, good, obedient to their own husbands, that the word of GOD be not blasphemed (Titus 2:3-5).

THE GIRLS' NIGHT OUT

First and foremost, when a woman is married, she isn't any longer considered a girl but a woman. Her first priority should be her family, and there is no longer me time but "we" time. The word "we" is used to implicate your husband and children, if you have any.

As a wife, you must practice being a keeper at home. Regardless of whether or not you are employed, your duties consist of caring for the needs of your household, which can get very hectic. But if you're dedicating maximum effort toward fulfilling the needs of your family, you really will be too exhausted to hang out with your girlfriends. If you enjoy having lunch with your girlfriends while your children are at school and your husband doesn't have an issue with it, then it's fine. However, being a married woman, you really shouldn't be hanging out all night or leaving your children with your husband for numerous hours, expecting him to perform your wifely duties while you're hanging out with your friends at a nightclub.

Don't get any misconceptions—your husband is expected to assist you in caring for the children, but only if you're ill or involved in something constructive. There really isn't any reason that a woman should be out late at night with the exception of school, work, or being accompanied by her husband. This behavior will instill values in your daughters and teach your sons the characteristics to seek in a woman.

A foolish woman is clamorous: she is simple, and knoweth nothing (Proverbs 9:13).

EVERY wise woman buildeth her house: but the foolish plucketh it down with her hands (Proverbs 14:1).

She is loud and stubborn; her feet abide not in her house: Now is she without, now in the streets, and lieth in wait at every corner. (Proverbs 7:11-12).

And the foolish said unto the wise, Give us of your oil; for our lamps are gone out (Matthew 25:8).

Forsake the foolish, and live; and go in the way of understanding (Proverbs 9:6).

It is a sport to a fool to do mischief: but a man of understanding hath wisdom (Proverbs 10:23).

He that troubleth his own house shall inherit the wind: and the fool shall be servant to the wise of heart (Proverbs 11:29).

He that refuseth instruction depiseth his own soul: but he that heareth reproof getteth understanding (Proverbs 15:32).

YOUR MOTHER-IN-LAW

Sometimes mothers-in-law can be nightmares. They usually desire to control their daughters-in-law and are often considered to be home invaders. Some mothers-in-law have made the lives of their daughters-in-law completely miserable in their efforts to maintain control of their sons. Even still, there shouldn't be any form of retaliation on your part, but instead, submission to prayer concerning the matter. To retaliate only complicates the problem.

You don't want to force your husband into choosing between his mother and his wife. Consider the possibility that both mothers (your mother and your spouse's mother) could be villains. Thus, regardless of your mother-in-law's behavior, you should always attempt to display love and kindness toward her. When your mother-in-law is being rude, don't get into an altercation with her. Listen, observe, ask questions, and keep negative responses to yourself.

To conclude, no matter how awful your mother-in-law is, do not put your upbringing in question. Take it to the Lord in *prayer,* because *prayer* changes circumstances as well as people!

For if ye love them which love you, what thank have ye? for sinners also love those that love them (Luke 6:32).

And I will sow her unto me in the earth; and I will have mercy upon her that had not obtained mercy; and I will say to them which were not my people, Thou art my people; and they shall say, Thou art my God (Hosea 2:23).

And this I pray, that your love may abound yet more and more in knowledge and in all judgment (Philippians 1:9).

And above all things have fervent charity among yourselves: for charity shall cover the multitude of sins (1 Peter 4:8).

But God, who is rich in mercy, for his great love wherewith he loved us (Ephesians 2:4).

A new commandment I give unto you, That ye love one another; as I have loved you, that ye also love one another. By this shall all men know that ye are my disciples, if ye have love one to another. (John13:34-35).

And the Lord make you to increase and abound in love one toward another, and toward all men, even as we do toward you (1 Thessalonians 3:12).

And we walk in love, as Christ also hath loved us, and hath given himself for us an offering and a sacrifice to God for a sweet-smelling savour (Ephesians 5:2).

Let love be without dissimulation. Abhor that which is evil; cleave to that which is good. Be kindly affectioned one to another with brotherly love; in honour preferring one another (Romans 12:9-10).

And hope maketh not ashamed; because the love of God is shed abroad in our hearts by the Holy Ghost which is given unto us (Romans 5:5).

Beloved, let us love one another: for love is of God; and every one that loveth is born of God, and knoweth God. He that loveth not knoweth not God; for God is love (1 John 4:7-8).

Let brotherly love continue (Hebrews 13:1).

But if any man love God, the same is known of him (1 Corinthians 8:3).

How excellent is thy lovingkindness, O God! Therefore the children of men put their trust under the shadow of thy wings (Psalm 36:7).

Because he hath set his love upon me, therefore will I deliver him: I will set him on high, because he hath known my name (Psalm 91:14).

PRODUCTIVITY

Women do not have to work a nine-to-five to be considered productive. In my opinion, productivity is simply making your time valuable. Therefore, a college student is productive. However, whether or not a woman chooses to work depends upon whether her husband is willing and able to support her financially or is willing to support her but is financially unable. If a man is unable to support his wife, then she should be working without question.

And the LORD God said, It is not good that man should be alone; I will make him an help meet for him. (Genesis 2:18).

According to the above biblical verse, God believed that the man should not be alone, and God sent the man a helper, which was woman. Therefore, a man should not be alone when he faces financial responsibility, because a woman must be at his side to help him meet the bills.

There are many legitimate ways that a woman can earn money that will aid in supporting her household—garage and bake sales, pre-sale dinners, sewing clothes, etc. If you don't need to spend your earnings immediately, simply find an old jar, place the money inside, and start an at-home savings account. In the future, you can use the money for the holidays or even a rainy day.

It really doesn't matter which job you choose to earn your wages as long as it's legitimate, and I encourage you to make your time valuable—after all, each second counts. If you are uncertain of what you can do to earn extra money but desire to do something, I advise you to *pray* and ask God to prosper your hands, as he did Joseph's hands (Genesis 39:3).

And the LORD God took the man, and put him into the garden of Eden to dress it and to keep it (Genesis 2:15).

The heart of her husband doth safely trust in her, so that he shall have no need of spoil (Proverbs 31:11).

Prepare thy work without, and make it fit for thyself in the field; and afterwards build thine house (Proverbs 24:27).

A good man leaveth an inheritance to his children's children: and the wealth of the sinner is laid up for the just (Proverbs 13:22).

And in the same house remain, eating and drinking such things as they give: for the labourer is worthy of his hire. Go not from house to house (Luke 10:7).

For which of you, intending to build a tower, sitteth not down first, and counteth the cost, whether he have sufficient to finish it? (Luke 14:28)

But let every man prove his own work, and then shall he have rejoicing in himself alone, and not in another. For every man shall bear his own burden (Galatians 6:4-5).

And that ye study to be quiet, and to do your own business, and to work with your own hands, as we commanded you (1 Thessalonians 4:11).

Let him that stole steal no more: but rather let him labour, working with his hands the thing which is good, that he may have to give to him that needeth (Ephesians 4:28).

For even when we were with you, this we commanded you, that if any would not work, neither should he eat (2 Thessalonians 3:10).

The thoughts of the diligent tend only to plenteousness; but of every one that is hasty only to want . . . There is a treasure to be desired and oil in the dwelling of the wise; but a foolish man spendeth it up (Proverbs 21:5, 20).

And the LORD was with Joseph, and he was a prosperous man; and he was in the house of his master the Egyptian; And his master saw that the LORD was with him, and that the LORD made all that he did to prosper in his hand. And Joseph found grace in his sight, and he served him: and he made him overseer over his house, and all that he had he put into his hand. And it came to pass from the time that he had made him overseer in his house, and over all that he had, that the LORD blessed the Egyptian's house for Joseph's sake; and the blessing of the LORD was upon all that he had in the house, and in the field. (Genesis 39:2-5).

In the sweat of thy face shalt thou eat bread, till thou return unto the ground; for out of it wast thou taken: for dust thou art, and unto dust shalt thou return (Genesis 3:19).

He becometh poor that dealeth with a slack hand: but the hand of the diligent maketh rich. The labour of the righteous tendeth to life: the fruit of the wicked to sin (Proverbs 10:4, 16).

The hand of the diligent shall bear rule: but the slothful shall be under tribute (Proverbs 12:24).

She will do him good and not evil all the days of her life . . . She considereth a field, and buyeth it: with the fruit of her hands she planteth a vineyard. She girdeth her loins with strength, and strengtheneth her arms . . . She layeth her hands to the spindle, and her hands hold the distaff. She maketh fine linen, and selleth it; and delivereth girdles unto the merchant . . . Strength and honour are her clothing; and she shall rejoice in time to come (Proverbs 31:12, 16-17, 19, 24-25).

Since the beginning of time, God has always lead by example.

And on the seventh day God ended his work which he had made; and he rested on the seventh day from all his work which he had made (Genesis 2:2).

If God can work, then shouldn't we, being made his likeness, be able to work, too?

PROVIDING FOR YOUR FAMILY

You should always be prepared in advance for anything that your family will need. Your kitchen should always be stocked with food and never empty. Medical and dental appointments should be up to date for each family member, as well as regular optometrist visits. You should always ensure that your family members are prepared with the clothing that they are going to need for each season of the year. Often when shopping for out-of-season items, you can get them at really low prices!

She is not afraid of the snow for her household: for all her household are clothed with scarlet . . . She looketh well to the ways of her household, and eateth not the bread of idleness (Proverbs 31:21, 27).

YOUR PRAYER LIFE

Always communicate with God, and never fail to include him in all that you do. It's wise to seek God prior to making certain decisions rather than making them on your own and regretting them later. Prayer is a request made by supplication and is a divine power given to you by God for the changing of your circumstances. It is your point of contact to God, who has armed you with the weapon of prayer to cancel and make null the plans of the enemy to destroy the lives of your family members and you.

Prayer is used as a covering of protection for each of your family members and you. Through the power of prayer, the sick have been healed, the lame have walked, the dead have risen, prisoners have been released, etc. I've often heard this saying: "A family that prays together stays together." Never discontinue the power of prayer in your home. The enemy, being fully aware of the power of prayer and fasting, diligently seeks to hinder and destroy your prayer life. It is extremely important that you cover your relationships with prayer, as the enemy is seeking to destroy them all.

Moreover as for me, God forbid that I should sin against the LORD in ceasing to pray for you: but I will teach you the good and the right way (1 Samuel 12:23).

If my people, which are called by my name, shall humble themselves, and pray, and seek my face, and turn from their wicked ways; then will I hear from heaven, and will forgive their sin, and will heal their land (2 Chronicles 7:14).

Evening, and morning, and at noon, will I pray, and cry aloud: and he shall hear my voice (Psalm 55:17).

But thou, when thou prayest, enter into thy closet, and when thou hast shut thy door, pray to thy FATHER which is in secret; and thy FATHER which seeth in secret shall reward thee openly. But when ye pray, use not vain repetitions, as the heathen do: for they think that they shall be heard for their much speaking (Matthew 6:6-7).

And it came to pass, that, as he was praying in a certain place, when he ceased, one of his disciples said unto him, LORD, teach us to pray, as John also taught his disciples (Luke 11:1).

And he spake a parable unto them to this end, that men ought always to pray, and not to faint.(Luke 18:1).

Likewise the spirit also helpeth our infirmities: for we know not what we should pray for as we ought: but the spirit itself maketh intercession for us with groanings which cannot be uttered (Romans 8:26).

Pray for us: for we trust we have a good conscience, in all things willing to live honestly (Hebrews 13:18).

Howbeit this kind goeth not out but by prayer and fasting (Matthew 17:21).

And all things, whatsoever ye shall ask in prayer, believing, ye shall receive (Matthew 21:22).

And when ye stand praying, forgive, if ye have ought against any: that your FATHER also which is in heaven may forgive you your trespasses (Mark 11:25).

Take ye heed, watch and pray: for ye know not when the time is (Mark 13:33).

Therefore said he unto them, The harvest truly is great, but the labourers are few: pray ye therefore the LORD of the harvest, that he would send forth labourers into his harvest (Luke 10:2).

Confess your faults one to another, and pray one for another, that ye may be healed. The effectual fervent prayer of a righteous man availeth much (James 5:16).

A WOMAN WHO FEARS THE LORD

A wise woman fears the Lord, and her fear of him assists in governing who she is. She maintains a high level of self-respect, is in full control of her actions, and diligently seeks God prior to her decision-making. Her desire is to always please the Lord in all things. She trusts in the Lord with all of her mind, heart, and soul. She places her flesh under subjection in order to remain faithful to the Lord. She allows the Lord to order her steps while avoiding unclean places and conversations. Each day of her life, she seeks the Lord by prayer and supplication. She is worthy of her husband's honor.

Like as a father pitieth his children, so the LORD pitieth them that fear him (Psalm 103:13).

The fear of the LORD is the beginning of knowledge: but fools despise wisdom and instruction (Proverbs 1:7).

Only fear the LORD, and serve him in truth with all your heart: for consider how great things he hath done for you (1 Samuel 12:24).

And he said, Lay not thine hand upon the lad, neither do thou any thing unto him: for now I know that thou fearest GOD, seeing thou hast not withheld thou son, thine only son from me (Genesis 22:12).

Favour is deceitful, and beauty is vain: but a woman that feareth the LORD, she shall be praised (Proverbs 31:30).

Trust in the LORD with all thine heart; and lean not unto thine own understanding. Be not wise in thine own eyes: fear the LORD, and depart from evil (Proverbs 3:5, 7).

Let us hear the conclusion of the whole matter: Fear GOD, and keep his commandments: for this is the whole duty of man (Ecclesiastes 12:13).

And fear not them which kill the body, but are not able to kill the soul: but rather fear him which is able to destroy both soul and body in hell (Matthew 10:28).

Honour all men. Love the brotherhood. Fear GOD. Honour the king (1 Peter 2:17).

The fear of the LORD is the beginning of wisdom: and the knowledge of the holy is understanding (Proverbs 9:10).

LOVE AND FORGIVENESS

According to *Webster's New Compact Dictionary,* the human heart is considered the center of emotions, personality, and attributes. The heart governs our thoughts, feelings, and emotions. It is the residence of love, hate, good, and evil. Knowing this, we must always keep our hearts pure.

Utilizing the tool of forgiveness is one way of maintaining a pure heart. According to Wikipedia, Forgiveness is typically defined as the process of concluding resentment, indignation, or anger as a result of a perceived offense, difference, or mistake or ceasing to demand restitution. Forgiveness isn't for the offender but for the forgiver. When the forgiver chooses to forgive the offender, it is an act of being set free from a hurtful past in which you are bound by the enemy in exchange for a more promising future in which you are liberated by God!

Hate is an act introduced by unforgiveness which hinders your relationship with God and your prayer life. Forgiveness promotes spiritual healing, a healthier life, and positive thinking. Forgiveness is responsible for introducing love into your life once again.

Love is God's greatest commandment. Love helps us to focus on the needs of an individual rather than his or her shortcomings. Love is a very powerful weapon that the enemy doesn't want in our possession. The act of one's love for another has prevented suicide attempts, sustained hope, healed the sick, fed and clothed the poor, etc. Love is so powerful that it goes beyond the grave. Think of someone who you love who is now deceased. Do you love that individual any less because he or she isn't any longer a part of your life? I strongly believe that your reply is *no.* As Bishop Lawrence always says, "Love is what it does!"

For from within, out of the heart of men, proceed evil thoughts, adulteries, fornications, murders, Thefts, covetousness, wickedness, deceit, lasciviousness, an evil eye, blasphemy, pride, foolishness: All these evil things come from within, and defile the man (Mark 7:21-23).

Thou shalt not avenge, nor bear any grudge against the children of thy people, but thou shalt love thy neighbor as thyself: I am the LORD (Leviticus 19:18).

And thou shalt love the LORD thy God with all thine heart, and with all thy soul, and with all thy might (Deuteronomy 6:5).

Hatred stirreth up strifes: but love covereth all sins (Proverbs 10:12).

Better is a dinner of herbs where love is, than a stalled ox and hatred therewith (Proverbs 15:17).

But I say unto you, Love your enemies, bless them that curse you, do good to them that hate you, and pray for them which despitefully use you, and persecute you (Matthew 5:44).

Love worketh no ill to his neighbor: therefore love is the fulfilling of the law (Romans 13:10).

And we have known and believed the love that God hath to us. God is love; and he that dwelleth in love dwelleth in God, and God in him. Herein is our love made perfect, that we may have boldness in the day of judgment: because as he is, so are we in this world. There is no fear in love; but perfect love casteth out fear: because fear hath torment. He that feareth is not made perfect in love. We love him, because he first loved us. If a man say, I love God, and hateth his brother, he is a liar: for he that loveth not his brother whom he hath seen, how can he love God whom he hath not seen? And this commandment have we from him, That he who loveth God love his brother also (1 John 4:16-21).

For if ye forgive men their trespasses, your heavenly Father will also forgive you. But if ye forgive not men their trespasses, neither will your Father forgive your trespasses (Matthew 6:14-15).

And be ye kind one to another, tenderhearted, forgiving one another, even as God for Christ's sake hath forgiven you (Ephesians 4:32).

Forbearing one another, and forgiving one another, if any man have a quarrel against any: even as Christ forgave you, so also do ye (Colossians 3:13).

A GENTLE AND QUIET SPIRIT

A man's home is his castle in which he is the king. His home is his place of refuge; it is also where he seeks to acquire love, comfort, and a peaceful environment. When a man enters his domain, the last thing that he expects to encounter is mayhem, especially when it's coming from his wife. A woman mustn't be argumentative, rude, or obnoxious. Instead, she must possess a gentle and quiet spirit.

Most men despise it when a woman is always arguing and consider her behavior to be annoying, aggravating, and nagging. Generally, most African-American and Hispanic women are guilty of this behavior, while the majority of Caucasian women are less confrontational. Often black men are ridiculed by black women for having interracial relationships, but we (black women) give our men reasons not to be interested in our race. I realize that there are some dominant women out there—and there isn't anything wrong with that—but start focusing on utilizing your strengths in areas that will help you to excel in life instead of hinder you.

Have you ever considered that men justify cheating by your constant nagging? And even worse, some men will intentionally do something that will annoy you to promote an argument so they have an excuse to leave home just to be with another woman. Therefore, the next time you feel the urge to nag, argue, or complain, simply take a breather, and begin to pray to God. Ask him to tame your tongue—even if he has to put a muzzle on your mouth!

Likewise, ye wives, be in subjection to your own husbands; that, if any obey not the word, they also may without the word be won by the conversation of the wives; While they behold your chaste conversation coupled with fear; Whose adorning let it not be that outward adorning of plaiting the hair, and of wearing of gold, or of putting on of apparel; But let it be the hidden man of the heart, in that which is not corruptible, even the ornament of a meek and quiet spirit, which is in the sight of God of great price. For after this manner in the old time the holy women also, who trusted in God, adorned themselves, being in subjection unto their own husbands: Even as Sara obeyed Abraham, calling him lord: whose daughters ye are, as long as ye do well, and are not afraid with any amazement (1 Peter 3:1-6).

But the fruit of the Spirit is love, joy, peace, longsuffering, gentleness, goodness, faith, Meekness, temperance: against such there is no law. And they that are Christ's have crucified the flesh with the affections and lusts. If we live in the Spirit, let us also walk in the Spirit. Let us not be desirous of vain glory, provoking one another, envying one another (Galatians 5:22-26).

For kings, and for all that are in authority; that we may lead a quiet and peaceable life in all godliness and honesty (1 Timothy 2:2).

Nevertheless let every one of you in particular so love his wife even as himself; and the wife see that she reverence her husband (Ephesians 5:33).

The mouth of a righteous man is a well of life: but violence covereth the mouth of the wicked. In the multitude of words there wanteth not sin: but he that refraineth his lips is wise. The lips of the righteous know what is acceptable: but the mouth of the wicked speaketh forwardness (Proverbs 10:11, 19, 32).

The beginning of strife is as when one letteth out water: therefore leave off contention, before it be meddled with. Even a fool, when he holdeth his peace, is counted wise: and he that shutteth his lips is esteemed a man of understanding (Proverbs 17:14, 28).

SHE IS A PEACEMAKER

A peacemaker is one who makes peace by settling quarrels, refuses to entertain gossip, and carefully selects her words. Everywhere that she goes, she brings her peace along with her; if her peace is rejected, she will depart, taking her peace with her. She overlooks rude remarks made by others in an effort to avoid any potential problems.

A peacemaker holds her peace in her marriage even if there is a problem and she is correct. She doesn't allow pride to interfere with her actions toward her spouse. She always speaks positively to her circumstances even when her home is in turmoil and the storms are raging in her life. She will hold her peace and trust God when she's aware that her spouse is involved in adulterous relationships, her children are misbehaving, and her finances are under the enemy's attack. She will speak life into her lifeless circumstances and refuse to allow the enemy to destroy her household.

She arises in the middle of the night while her household is asleep and begins to pray to the almighty God. She cries out to God for the changing of her circumstances and is comforted by her prayer. She begins to speak positively to her circumstances, and with God-given authority, she commands the enemy to depart from her home by saying, "Peace; be still."

THE TELEPHONE OR HELL PHONE?

Women, please be aware that it's difficult for a man to respect his wife when she spends the majority of her time gossiping about someone else's situation. Generally, when a woman conducts herself in this matter, it is an indicator that she's unhappy within. You always want to protect your character and never allow anyone to take you outside of your element.

Therefore, it's always best to avoid foolishness. Whenever you're on the telephone, it should be for business purposes, encouraging another, or casual conversation, but it should never be to discredit another individual or worry about someone else's affairs. Sometimes meddlers need peace within themselves in order to prevent worrying about others. Believe it or not, inner peace sometimes helps us to avoid foolishness.

Peace I leave with you, my peace I give unto you: not as the world giveth, give I unto you. Let not your heart be troubled, neither let it be afraid (John 14:27).

Blessed are the peacemakers: for they shall be called the children of God (Matthew 5:9).

And if the house be worthy, let your peace come upon it: but if it be not worthy, let your peace return to you (Matthew 10:13).

THEREFORE being justified by faith, we have peace with GOD through our Lord Jesus Christ (Romans 5:1).

For kings, and for all that are in authority; that we may lead a quiet and peaceable life in all godliness and honesty (1 Timothy 2:2).

And whosoever shall not receive you, nor hear you, when ye depart thence, shake off the dust under your feet for a testimony against them. Verily I say unto you, It shall be more tolerable for Sodom and Gomor'-rha in the day of judgment, than for that city (Mark 6:11).

Follow peace with all men, and holiness, without which no man shall see the LORD (Hebrews 12:14).

And the peace of God, which passeth all understanding, shall keep your hearts and minds through Christ Jesus . . . Those things, which ye have both learned, and received, and heard, and seen in me, do: and the God of peace shall be with you (Philippians 4:7, 9).

MEEKNESS AND PATIENCE

According to *Webster's New Compact Dictionary,* meekness is displaying patience and a gentle disposition, mild and easily imposed on, or often considered not to have any backbone. Yet being meek doesn't mean that you are weak; instead, it demonstrates your faith in God to fulfill his promises.

Patience is also an aspect of being meek. No man can be made strong unless he first endures the law of patience. Therefore, you must not become weary while waiting on God to fulfill his promises. Often when we're praying for a certain situation or an individual, it sometimes seems as if God isn't going to answer our prayers.

When a loved one is battling an addiction and you're exhausting every effort not to give up on that individual or prevent saying anything to the individual which may possibly hinder his or her progress, situations appear to become the more difficult. It is during those times that it seems that the prayer line is inoperable, and you really wish that you could go directly to God (face to face) just to inquire about the delay. During those times, your patience is needful and should be activated.

What is patience? According to Webster's New Compact Dictionary, Patience is calm tolerance of delay without complaining. As the almighty God lives, he shall certainly deliver his blessings as he has promised. However, you must patiently await your appointed season while holding steadfast to your faith. Remember, Rome wasn't built in a day!

Blessed are the meek: for they shall inherit the earth (Matthew 5:5).

The meek also shall increase their joy in the LORD, and the poor among men shall rejoice in the Holy One of Israel (Isaiah 29:19).

The LORD lifteth up the meek: He casteth the wicked down to the ground (Psalm 147:6).

For the LORD taketh pleasure in his people: he will beautify the meek with salvation (Psalm 149:4).

Knowing this, that the trying of your faith worketh patience (James 1:3).

To every thing there is a season, and a time to every purpose under the heaven (Ecclesiastes 3:1).

And not only so, but we glory in tribulations also: knowing that tribulation worketh patience. And patience, experience; and experience, hope (Romans 5:3-4).

WHEREFORE seeing we also are compassed about with so great a cloud of witnesses, let us lay aside every weight, and the sin which doth so easily beset us, and let us run with patience the race that is set before us (Hebrews 12:1).

And to knowledge temperance; and to temperance patience; and to patience godliness (2 Peter 1:6).

CHARITY

According to *Webster's New Compact Dictionary,* charity is having love for all of mankind, leniency in judging others, and generosity toward the needy. According to the Bible, even if you possess all gifts, if you do not have charity, you are nothing. Charity overlooks the faults of others and always assists them in fulfilling their needs. Charity is opening your heart to those who are in need.

Charity doesn't always have to be in the form of money or material things. Sometimes charity can be as simple as being a listening ear to someone who needs to share his or her problems. Sometimes just being there for someone is of more value than money. Charity comes from within the heart and is a gift that cannot be hidden.

If you have charity, it will always be expressed among those around you as well as those who are fortunate to come in contact with you. Unfortunately, many people believe that when God blesses them, it's only to benefit themselves and their families. This is not so. Many times, God blesses us so that we may be a blessing to others.

Be not forgetful to entertain strangers: for thereby some have entertained angels unawares (Hebrews 13:2).

Though I speak with the tongues of men and of angels, and have not charity, I am become as sounding brass, or a tinkling cymbal . . . And though I bestow all my goods to feed the poor, and though I give my body to be burned, and have not charity, it profiteth me nothing. Charity suffereth long, and is kind; charity envieth not; charity vaunteth not itself, is not puffed up . . . And now abideth faith, hope, charity, these three; but the greatest of these is charity (1 Corinthians 13:1, 3-4, 13).

And to godliness brotherly kindness; and to brotherly kindness charity (2 Peter 1:7).

Flee also youthful lusts: but follow righteousness, faith, charity, peace, with them that call on the Lord out of a pure heart (2 Timothy 2:22).

That the aged men be sober, grave, temperate, sound in faith, in charity, in patience (Titus 2:2).

Blessed is he that considereth the poor: the LORD will deliver him in time of trouble (Psalm 41:1).

I have been young, and now am old; yet have I not seen the righteous forsaken, nor his seed begging bread (Psalm 37:25).

He that hath pity upon the poor lendeth unto the LORD; and that which he hath given will he pay him again (Proverbs 19:17).

He hath dispersed, he hath given to the poor; his righteousness endureth for ever; his horn shall be exalted with honour (Psalm 112:9).

FAITH

According to *Webster's New Compact Dictionary,* faith is unquestioning belief and complete trust—specifically in God. You must totally trust in God with all of your heart, mind, and soul no matter the nature or severity of the problem. Faith is believing that you are healed even when doctors have diagnosed you with an illness. Faith is believing that God can do all things but fail.

Exercising your faith makes a difference in your circumstances. You can't expect God to move in your circumstances if you doubt that he has the power to change them. You must first believe that God is who he is and that all power is in his hands.

But let him ask in faith, nothing wavering. For he that wavereth is like a wave of the sea driven with the wind and tossed. For let not that man think that he shall receive any thing of the Lord (James 1:6-7).

But without faith it is impossible to please him: for he that cometh to God must believe that he is, and that he is a rewarder of them that diligently seek him (Hebrews 11:6).

That your faith should not stand in the wisdom of men, but in the power of God (1 Corinthians 2:5).

We having the same spirit of faith, according as it is written, I believed, and therefore have I spoken; we also believe, and therefore speak (2 Corinthians 4:13).

Therefore we conclude that a man is justified by faith without the deeds of the law (Romans 3:28).

I am crucified with Christ: nevertheless I live; yet not I, but Christ liveth in me: and the life which I now live in the flesh I live by the faith of the Son of God, who loved me, and gave himself for me (Galatians 2:20).

What doth it profit, my brethren, though a man say he hath faith, and have not works? Can faith save him? Even so faith, if it hath not works, is dead, being alone. Yea, a man may say, Thou hast faith, and I have works: shew me thy faith without thy works, and I will shew thee my faith by my works (James 2:14, 17-18).

So then faith cometh by hearing, and hearing by the word of God (Romans 10:17).

Now faith is the substance of things hoped for, the evidence of things not seen (Hebrews 11:1).

And Jesus said unto them, Because of your unbelief: for verily I say unto you, If ye have faith as a grain of a mustard seed, ye shall say unto this mountain, Remove hence to yonder place; and it shall remove; and nothing shall be impossible unto you (Matthew 17:20).

TAKING GOOD CARE OF YOURSELF

It does not matter what your dress size is; you should always look your best to impress yourself and your husband. However, if you're uncomfortable with something about yourself, then by all means, change it. The world has much to offer in terms of beauty. There are many options available to assist you in achieving your goals.

No matter what you decide, just be content with your decision, and make sure that you're improving your body to please yourself and no one else. No matter how big or small you are, learn to embrace yourself, because you are *beautiful* and *unique!*

Always keep routine doctor's visits to ensure good health. It is important that you eat healthy food, drink lots of water, and exercise. Ensure that you maintain the proper rest, and try not to worry. If you have a problem that you can't resolve, talk with your pastor, and take it to God in prayer—but leave it there with God.

Remember that maintaining good health is your responsibility, and worrying isn't good for your health. Also, take proper care of your skin; routine facials assist in maintaining youthful skin. Regular dental appointments are needful, as you always want to maintain a beautiful smile. Massages are great if you're a bit stressed. A bikini wax enhances your appearance in your lingerie. Regular pedicures and manicures are also important for your appearance.

If you can afford it, try to visit your hairstylist at least once a week, and be diversified by trying new hair colors and different hairstyles. I'm sure your husband will enjoy your new look as long as it's appropriate. You should always ensure that you look your best in the public. The virtuous woman looked well to the ways of her household, but she took care of herself as well!

I will praise thee; for I am fearfully and wonderfully made: marvelous are thy works; and that my soul knoweth right well (Psalm 139:14).

He that getteth wisdom loveth his own soul: he that keepeth understanding shall find good (Proverbs 19:8).

She maketh herself coverings of tapestry; her clothing is silk and purple (Proverbs 31:22).

What? Know ye not that your body is the temple of the Holy Ghost Which is in you, which ye have of God, and ye are not your own? For ye are bought with a price: therefore glorify God in your body, and in your spirit, which are God's (1 Corinthians 6:19-20).

Beloved, I wish above all things that thou mayest prosper and be in health, even as thy soul prospereth (3 John 1:2).

Know ye not that ye are the temple of God, and that the spirit of God dwelleth in you (1 Corinthians 3:16).

Is any sick among you? let him call for the elders of the church; and let them pray over him, anointing him with oil in the name of the LORD (James 5:14).

For I will restore health unto thee, and I will heal thee of thy wounds, saith the LORD; because they called thee an Outcast, saying, This is Zion, whom no man seeketh after (Jeremiah 30:17).

Behold, I will bring it health and cure, and I will cure them, and will reveal unto them the abundance of peace and truth (Jeremiah 33:6).

Chapter Three

HIS INFIDELITY

If your husband has ever been unfaithful it must have been very devastating for you and quite difficult to overcome. The hurt that you may have endured is indescribable, and the pain is unbearable. These feelings are normal, as you have been betrayed by someone who you love dearly. You trusted him with everything you owned, including your heart. You were terribly embarrassed and emotionally scarred. You may have cried until your eyes totally denied your request to produce any more tears.

You've asked yourself why more than one thousand times. All you can imagine is him making love to another woman as he has made love to you. And much worse, you begin to ask yourself, "What if he made love to her better than he made love to me?" You've promised yourself not to allow your children to observe your pain, but somehow, you can't control your emotions. And, unfortunately, the children manage to witness you an emotional wreck!

You may have experienced countless sleepless nights that were caused by your pain. Each day, you may have asked yourself, "How could he do this to me?" You may have made several attempts to find out why was he unfaithful to you, but each time, he avoided the question or answered you indirectly. You may feel as if everything that you've worked so diligently to build has been instantly taken away from you overnight.

You may begin to question God, and your anger may kindle inside of you like a burning building. If you aren't extremely cautious, it is possible that depression, anxiety, or suicidal spirits can enter inside of you. If you are experiencing this pain or have experienced this pain but aren't over it, I advise you to diligently seek God through prayer and fasting, as God is an emotional healer!

The sacrifices of God are a broken spirit: a broken and a contrite heart, O God, thou wilt not despise (Psalm 51:17).

My heart is smitten, and withered like grass; so that I forget to eat my bread (Psalm 102:4).

From the end of the earth will I cry unto thee, when my heart is overwhelmed: lead me to the rock that is higher than I (Psalm 61:2).

My heart panteth, my strength faileth me: as for the light of mine eyes, it also is gone from me (Psalm 38:10).

HEAR my cry, O GOD; attend unto my prayer (Psalm 61:1).

The LORD is nigh unto them that are of a broken heart; and saveth such as be of a contrite spirit (Psalm 34:18).

Cast thy burden upon the LORD, and he shall sustain thee: he shall never suffer the righteous to be moved (Psalm 55:22).

My flesh and my heart faileth: but God is the strength of my heart, and my portion for ever . . . But it is good for me to draw near to God: I have put my trust in the LORD God, that I may declare all thy works (Psalm 73:26, 28).

He healeth the broken in heart, and bindeth up their wounds (Psalm 147:3).

He sent his word, and healed them, and delivered them from their destructions (Psalm 107:20).

And whatsoever ye shall ask in my name, that will I do, that the Father may be glorified in the son (John 14:13).

And he said unto me, My grace is sufficient for thee: for my strength is made perfect in weakness. Most gladly therefore will I rather glory in my infirmities, that the power of Christ may rest upon me (2 Corinthians 12:9).

Fear thou not; for I am with thee: be not dismayed; for I am thy God: I will strengthen thee; yea, I will help thee; yea, I will uphold thee with the right hand of my righteousness (Isaiah 41:10).

And we know that all things work together for good to them that love God, to them who are the called according to his purpose (Romans 8:28).

SEEKING ADVICE

Many times, when we're in emotional distress, we seek someone to be our listening ear. We even seek advice from others—which isn't generally a problem, depending upon who we're seeking the advice from. When a woman is married, it isn't wise for her to seek advice from a single woman, nor is it wise to seek advice from an ungodly woman.

You may know an older Christian woman who has been married for years, but you have to be certain as to how she feels about her husband as well as how well she treats him before you can seek her advice. Unfortunately, many young women have been advised by older women to date other men when their spouses have been unfaithful. Therefore, godly counsel is all you need!

You must be careful not to disclose information concerning your marriage to everyone—especially men. There have been many women who have committed adultery in a vulnerable state by confiding in other men concerning their marital problems. If you complain to another man about the things that your husband isn't doing, shouldn't do, or wouldn't do, quite naturally, he (the guy you're speaking with) would portray the image that you are obviously seeking for in a man. A man would go to the extreme to make you feel like brand new money, but the moment he makes love to you, he will proudly introduce to you his *real* self. Unfortunately, you will discover that he's no better than your husband. In fact, he's actually a lot worse than your husband in every aspect—including sex!

Don't search for love when it's obvious that you're heartbroken, vulnerable, lonely, and desperate, because there are many heartless men out there who prey on woman who are in this condition. Don't allow it to be *you!*

BLESSED is the man that walketh not in the counsel of the ungodly, nor standeth in the way of sinners, nor sitteth in the seat of the scornful (Psalm 1:1).

The LORD bringeth the counsel of the heathen to nought: he maketh the devices of the people of none effect (Psalm 33:10).

The counsel of the LORD standeth for ever, the thoughts of his heart to all generations (Psalm 33:11).

There are many devices in a man's heart; nevertheless the counsel of the LORD, that shall stand (Proverbs 19:21).

For I have not shunned to declare unto you all the counsel of God (Acts 20:27).

The aged women likewise, that they be in behavior as becometh holiness, not false accusers, not given to much wine, teachers of good things; That they may teach the young women to be sober, to love their husbands, to love their children (Titus 2:3-4).

In thee, O LORD, do I put my trust: let me never be put to confusion (Psalm 71:1).

IT'S YOUR DECISION

After infidelity, whether you choose to remain in the marriage or not, it's your decision alone. No one other than your pastors should give you any input or suggestions concerning the matter. I agree that divorce is always a difficult decision to make, but the decision of whether to divorce is one that you have to decide on your own, as you're the only one who has to live with your choices.

Although you may be disappointed in your husband, you must not allow anyone to bash him in your presence, because you are still married and are one flesh. I know it doesn't feel that way, but you are! Besides, hearing others bash him will only make you feel worse. Everyone should respect the tough decisions that you are facing during those difficult times and shouldn't impose.

Don't make irrational decisions based upon your emotions, as you also have to consider what is best for your children, if you have any. There isn't any need to expedite the divorce, so take as much time as you need to fast, pray, and wait on an answer from God concerning the matter. In conclusion, you must not allow the feelings of your family and friends to influence your decision to remain in the marriage or divorce.

Trust in the LORD with all thine heart; and lean not unto thine own understanding (Proverbs 3:5).

Though he slay me, yet will I trust in him: but I will maintain mine own ways before him (Job 13:15).

Cause me to hear thy lovingkindness in the morning; for in thee do I trust: cause me to know the way wherein I should walk; for I lift up my soul unto thee (Psalm 143:8).

He trusted in God; let him deliver him now, if he will have him: for he said, I am the Son of God (Matthew 27:43).

Thus saith the LORD; Cursed be the man that trusteth in man, and maketh flesh his arm, and whose heart departeth from the LORD (Jeremiah 17:5).

KEEPING YOURSELF

Regardless to what your husband has done or is doing, you must maintain your self-respect as a woman. You must realize that you can never repay your husband for what he's done to hurt you. Your decision to be unfaithful to your unfaithful husband isn't justified, for on your wedding day, you made a vow to be faithful until separated by death, and God expects you to remain committed to your vows even if your husband doesn't. When you stand before God to be judged, you will stand alone. Therefore, you should live to please God and not man.

Furthermore, your intimacy with another man, if discovered, could possibly affect your husband to a certain degree, but someday he would get over the emotional pain caused by your unfaithfulness. However, your decision to defile your body before the almighty God is one that you will have to live with forever. A God-fearing woman allows three men to view her nakedness—God, her husband, and her gynecologists! If you learn to love God more than you love your husband, when your husband fails you, it won't be so easy for you to give in to another man.

Women must learn to live inspirational lives. If you can keep yourself while experiencing the hurt of your husband's infidelity, chances are that God will enable you to encourage another woman to keep herself if she experiences her husband being unfaithful. Whenever you are tempted by the enemy to conduct yourself in a manner that is contrary to the Word of God, please remember that you are so much more than what the enemy allows you to see. Resist the devil, and then he will flee!

As a woman, you must uphold your standards, and as a Christian, you must uphold your reputation, for you neither live nor die unto yourself. Someday, someone's life will be touched by the life that you have chosen to live. Be encouraged! As a child of God, you have the victory! So even if it appears that you are defeated by the enemy, continue to praise God! And if for any reason, you feel defeated, I advise you to begin praising God until you feel the victory!

For whatsoever is born of God overcometh the world: and this is the victory that overcometh the world, even our faith. Who is he that overcometh the world, but he that beliveth that Jesus is the Son of God? (1 John 5:4-5)

Pure religion and undefiled before God and the Father is this, To visit the fatherless and widows in their affliction, and to keep himself unspotted from the world (James 1:27).

Jesus answered and said unto him, If a man love me, he will keep my words: and my Father will love him, and we will come unto him, and make our abode with him (John 14:23).

And the peace of God, which passeth all understanding, shall keep your hearts and minds through Christ Jesus (Philippians 4:7).

Thou wilt keep him in perfect peace, whose mind is stayed on thee: because he trusted in thee (Isaiah 26:3).

Know ye not that ye are the temple of God, and that the Spirit of God dwelleth in you? If any man defile the temple of God, him shall God destroy; for the temple of God is holy, which temple ye are (1 Corinthians 3:16-17).

This I say then, Walk in the Spirit, and ye shall not fulfil the lust of the flesh . . . Now the works of the flesh are manifest, which are these; Adultery, fornication, uncleaness, lasciviousness . . . And they that are Christ's have crucified the flesh with the affections and lusts (Galatians 5:16, 19, 24).

That which is gone out of thy lips thou shalt keep and perform; even a freewill offering, according as thou hast vowed unto the LORD thy God, which thou hast promised with thou mouth (Deuteronomy 23:23).

Submit yourselves therefore to God. Resist the devil, and he will flee from you (James 4:7).

RECONCILING YOUR MARRIAGE

Restoring a marriage that has been damaged by infidelity requires maximum effort, but if both partners are willing to work on restoration and are in love with each other, it can be accomplished. The key to emotional healing is letting go of your past in order to grab a hold to your future. Once you've discussed the problem between each other and received marital counseling (if needed), you must move toward the healing process. Dwelling on your hurtful past interferes with your healing process.

Your husband's act of infidelity doesn't relieve you of your wifely duties; God still requires you to continue to cook, clean, and satisfy your husband intimately. But under the circumstances, you should consider utilizing a form of protection (condoms) until he has been medically cleared of any sexually transmitted diseases. You must also respect your husband and his God-given authority without using his infidelity as a weapon of self-defense.

Don't live your life to please others; after infidelity many marriages that should have been restored weren't restored, because the wife feared what others would think concerning her decision to remain in her marriage. However, marriage is very serious and involves your future; therefore, it isn't about what others think, but what's best for you. You have to live with your decision forever, so you must decide what is in your best interest. If you desire your marriage, you must seek God for restoration.

And he shall be unto thee a restorer of thy life, and a nourisher of thine old age: for thy daughter in law, which loveth thee, which is better to thee than seven sons, hath born him (Ruth 4:15).

And it came to pass, as he was telling the king how he had restored a dead body to life, that, behold, the woman, whose son he had restored to life, cried to the king for her house and for her land. And Ge-ha'-zi said, My lord, O king, this is the woman, and this is her son, whom E-li'-sha restored to life. And when the king asked the woman, she told him. So the king appointed unto her a certain officer, saying, Restore all that was her's, and all the fruits of the field since the day that she left the land, even until now (2 Kings 8:5-6).

He restoreth my soul: he leadeth me in the paths of righteousness for his name's sake (Psalm 23:3).

Restore unto me the joy of thy salvation; and uphold me with thy free spirit (Psalm 51:12).

And they that shall be of thee shall build the old waste places: thou shalt raise up the foundations of many generations; and thou shalt be called, The repairer of the breach, The restorer of paths to dwell in (Isaiah 58:12).

Then said they, We will restore them, and will require nothing of them; so will we do as thou sayest. Then I called the priests, and took an oath of them, that they should do according to this promise (Nehemiah 5:12).

They shall be carried to Babylon, and there shall they be until the day that I visit them, saith the LORD; then will I bring them up, and restore them to this place (Jeremiah 27:22).

For I will restore health unto thee, and I will heal thee of thy wounds, saith the LORD; because they called thee an outcast saying, This is Zion, whom no man seeketh after (Jeremiah 30:17).

HOW TO FORGIVE AFTER INFIDELITY

The road to forgiveness begins by first admitting that your heart has been broken and then being willing to let go of your hurtful past. Realize that you are a survivor rather than a victim. Also, you must not view your marriage for what you think it should have been but for what it is. Realizing that we're all subject to human error is another step toward forgiveness.

Fervent prayer and fasting will aid in escaping the negative effects of hate, hurt, anger, and betrayal that were introduced by infidelity. In addition, putting forth maximum effort not to judge your husband or the situation is also a key factor in emotional healing. Judging only makes matters worse. You will benefit tremendously from the act of forgiveness, as forgiveness isn't for the offender but the forgiver.

THE KEY

According to the Bible, marriage is a binding contract between a male and female who, through unity, become one. There are several terms to this non-negotiable contract that must be honored, and the realization of marriage must be understood. First of all, every marriage will experience difficulties. In addition, you must build a relationship with God that will withstand the forces of evil. A good practice is to never go to bed with an unresolved problem.

This brings to my attention a quote from Bishop Austin Lawrence, concerning a married couple who had an argument. They went to bed without resolving their differences of opinions, and the husband passed away in his sleep. Due to the fact that the differences were not resolved, the wife became emotional and could never find closure after his death. Thus, all marriages are not perfect, and the forces of evil will always find their way, but a strong relationship with God will always bring you closure.

Be ye angry, and sin not: let not the sun go down upon your wrath: Neither give place to the devil (Ephesians 4:26, 27).

Chapter Four

SINGLE WOMEN DATING MARRIED MEN

Single women dating married men have become very common in today's society. Although God specifically speaks against adulterous relationships, most women have chosen to rebel against the Word of God to fulfill the lusts of the flesh. Women are entering relationships, aware that the men are married. In fact, dating a married man has become preferable to dating a single man among most women. I'm actually appauled to learn that most women consider this an option.

Women who indulge in these affairs must realize that dating a married man makes them indecent, and while they are considered dessert, the wives are the main course. Most women who indulge in this lifestyle are afraid of commitment and usually have more than one sex partner. In my opinion, married men who cheat are afraid of confronting the problems in their marriages. The married men are afraid of speaking to their wives in an effort to resolve any existing marital issues.

Therefore, in a married man's attempt to escape reality, the woman is used as a form of escapism or a random chick. A woman who has a relationship with a married man allows herself to become nothing more than entertainment to him. In fact, most married men enjoy having sex with their random chicks, because the men usually don't handle them appropriately or with care in bed. The men usually desire sexual favors that they wouldn't dare request from their respectable wives.

Married men also never feel obligated to their random chicks. More likely than not, all the promises they have ever made will never come to fruition. How many times does a married man promise to leave his wife and never does? The truth is that he wants to have his cake and eat it, too. How would you like to be in his wife's shoes? Would you like it if your husband were unfaithful to you? No one deserves to be treated in this manner.

Those who subscribe to a cheating lifestyle are guilty of contributing to the destruction of homes, children, and marriages. They are guilty of many, many broken hearts, including those of young children. These women cause many women to suffer tremendous heartache and pain. In their selfish, desperate attempt to find emotional connection, they are ruining the lives of many others.

Anyone who indulges in this lifestyle has absolutely no regard for the Word of God or another woman's marriage. In my opinion, any woman who seeks a relationship with a married man suffers from low self-esteem, is indecent, and is desperate. Otherwise, why would she waste her time when she can never build a home upon another woman's foundation, and why settle for a city when God can give her the entire world?

Women willingly indulge in this lifestyle, but when the relationship doesn't go as planned, they publicize their secret in an attempt to destroy their ex-lovers' marriages while portraying the victim. Unfortunately, society accepts this behavior, so it aids in the foolishness of these women by continuing to paint them as victims when they're actually the villains. In my opinion, there is only one victim in an act of infidelity, and that is the wife—sorry!

Be not deceived; God is not mocked: for whatsoever a man soweth, that shall he also reap (Galatians 6:7).

Therefore shall a man leave his father and his mother, and shall cleave unto his wife: and they shall be one flesh (Genesis 2:24).

Wherefore they are no more twain, but one flesh. What therefore God hath joined together, let not man put asunder (Matthew 19:6).

Nevertheless to avoid fornication, let every man have his own wife, and let every woman have her own husband (1 Corinthians 7:2).

Ye have heard that it was said by them of old time, Thou shalt not commit adultery (Matthew 5:27).

Thou knowest the commandments, Do not commit adultery, Do not kill, Do not steal, Do not bear false witness, Honour thy father and thy mother (Luke 18:20).

Now the works of the flesh are manifest, which are these; Adultery, fornication, uncleaness, lasciviousness (Galatians 5:19).

Husbands, love your wives, even as Christ also loved the church, and gave himself for it . . . So ought men to love their wives as their own bodies. He that loveth his wife loveth himself (Ephesians 5:25, 28).

KNOWING WHO YOU ARE IN CHRIST

God saw that Adam (man) was without a helper, and he caused a great sleep to fall upon him, and while he slept, God took one of his ribs and closed up his flesh. God then took that very same rib of which he (God) removed from Adam and created a woman (Eve), and he called her "woman," because she was taken from man. Woman was created not to walk behind or before man but beside man, and her purpose is to be his helper.

A man must respect your God-given purpose. You were uniquely designed by God in character and body structure and then presented as a gift from God to man. You were presented to be loved by your man and to be his strength, not to be lied to, verbally or emotionally abused, misused, taken advantage of, or trampled upon by man. You are your prize possession, and you don't need a man to define who you are. You don't have to settle for less (a married man) when you can have the best (your very own man).

Most women settle for any type of man when they are lonely. Have you heard the saying, "A piece of man is better than no man at all"? Well, I beg to differ! If I'm going to suffer in a relationship, it's going to be with the man that God has given me for a husband and not anyone else's husband. Why should I bear another woman's burdens? If he isn't any good for her, then he certainly wouldn't be any good for me!

When you decide to become involved in any relationship, you must seek God first through prayer and fasting. When you make your request known unto God, you must be specific concerning the characteristics you are looking for in a man. Please ensure that you request that he's honest. After all, you don't want him to claim that he's single only to learn later that he's actually married. You must be patient in all things—especially relationships. Ruth carefully and patiently sought Boaz, who was a successful businessman who feared God. Boaz was a noble man who made provision for both Ruth and her mother-in-law. Boaz referred to Ruth as a virtuous woman, which is an indication that he respected the woman she was.

When you decide to date a man, you mustn't lower your standards to become involved with him; he should raise the bar in order to be with you! You should always want to be recognized as a respectful woman who people refer to as virtuous. In order for a man to even consider you as wife material, you must present yourself as one who possesses morals and values as well as conduct yourself as a woman with class without substitution. Now tell the church *amen!*

And Na-o'-mi had a kinsman of her husband's, a mighty man of wealth, of the family of E-lim'-e-lech; and his name was Bo'-az . . . Then said Bo'-az unto Ruth, Hearest thou not, my daughter? Go not to glean in another field, neither go from hence, but abide her fast by my maidens: Let thine eyes be on the field that they do reap, and go thou after them: have I not charged the young men that they shall not touch thee? And when thou art athirst, go unto the vessels, and drink of that which the young men have drawn. Then she fell on her face, and bowed herself to the ground, and said unto him, Why have I found grace in thine eyes, that thou shouldest take knowledge of me, seeing I am a stranger? And Bo'-az answered and said unto her, It hath fully been shewed me, all that thou hast done unto thy mother in law since the death of thine husband: and how thou hast left thy father and thy mother, and the land of thy nativity, and art come unto a people which thou knewest not heretofore. The LORD recompense thy work, and a full reward be given thee of the LORD God of Israel, under whose wings thou art come to trust. Then she said, Let me find favour in thy sight, my lord; for that thou hast comforted me, and for that thou hast spoken friendly unto thine handmaid, though I be not like unto one of thine handmaidens. And Bo'-az said unto her, At mealtime come thou hither, and eat of the bread, and dip thy morsel in the vinegar. And she sat beside the reapers: and he reached her parched corn, and she did eat, and was sufficed, and left. And when she was risen up to glean, Bo'-az commanded his young men, saying, Let her glean even among the sheaves, and reproach her not: And let fall also some of the handfuls of purpose for her, and leave them, that she may glean them, and rebuke her not (Ruth 2:1, 8-16).

And when Bo'-az had eaten and drunk, and his heart was merry, he went to lie down at the end of the heap of corn: and she came softly, and uncovered his feet, and laid her down. And it came to pass at midnight, that the man was afraid, and turned himself: and, behold, a woman lay at his feet. And he said, Who art thou? And she answered, I am Ruth thine handmaid: spread therefore thy skirt over thine handmaid; for thou art a near kinsman. And he said, Blessed be thou of the LORD, my daughter: for thou hast shewed more kindness in the latter end than at the beginning, in as much as thou followedst not young men, whether poor or rich (Ruth 3:7-10).

And she lay at his feet until the morning: and she rose up before one could know another. And he said, Let it not be known that a woman came into the floor. Also he said, Bring the vail that thou hast upon thee, and hold it. And when she held it, he measured six measures of barley, and laid it on her: and she went into the city. And when she came to her mother in law, she said, Who art thou, my daughter? And she told her all that the man had done to her. And she said, These six measures of barley gave he me; for he said to me, Go not empty unto thy mother in law (Ruth 3:14-17).

Moreover Ruth the Mo'-ab-i-tess, the wife of Mah'-lon, have I purchased to be my wife, to raise up the name of the dead upon his inheritance, that the name of the dead be not cut off from among his brethren, and from the gate of his place: ye are witnesses this day (Ruth 4:10).

Boaz's decision not to send Ruth back to her mother-in-law empty-handed is proof that he was a man who made provision for his household. In today's society, many men are searching for women who are willing to provide for them (the men). More and more men are neglecting to conduct their duties as providers of their households.

Women, you were created by God to be a helper to your husband, but God never intended for you to become the sole providers in your home. As a woman, you must *stop* cheating yourself out of the promises of God. *Stop* becoming involved with married, emotionally or physically abusive, or freeloading men. If you are currently involved in any of the above relationships, please seek God for the courage to end it *now!* Why should you settle for a city when God can give you the entire world?

You and others like you who support men financially in exchange for sex are considered to be lower than a snake's belly and an insult to women. I can't even refer to women who behave in this matter as whores, because whores are compensated for their services, and these women are obviously not! The Bible described Gomer as a whore, yet Hosea compensated her—are these women any less than Gomer?

Don't get any misconceived notions, as I'm not promoting prostitution. However, I am suggesting that women consider their options when choosing a lifelong mate, because if a woman is dating a guy who refuses or can't contribute to her financial needs, then chances are that the situation will remain the same if not worsen once they are married. You must always bear in mind that it is much easier to support yourself than it is someone else and yourself. All women must realize that financially supporting men makes them appear lonely and desperate for sex and is degrading to all women.

Imagine this: A young woman is dating a young man who is unemployed. The young woman resides with her parents and is forbidden to have overnight visitors. Therefore, in an effort to spend quality time with her boyfriend, she purchases a hotel for one night and picks him up in her vehicle. They go to her favorite restaurant and she pays the bill, and tips the waitress. What is wrong with this scenario other than the fact that the young lady is indulging in the act of fornication (premarital sex)?

First of all, women should never consider becoming involved with men who are financially incapable of meeting the least of their needs. The following issue is that the young woman has entered into a relationship as the sole provider. And the sad part of it is that she's paying the cost of a hotel in effort to give herself to him sexually, but if he were interested in her, he would take the responsibility of paying the bill.

Please note that relationships usually end up in the way that they begin. Therefore, when you are employed, you must consider dating a guy who is also employed. If not, the two of you will be considered unequally yoked. I would like to clarify that if your husband hasn't been anything less than a provider for his family and for any reason he loses employment, as his wife, you must provide for your household without complaining until he's able to find employment again. In the meantime, your husband must not become complacent and should seek employment daily until he's successful in landing himself a job.

Be ye not unequally yoked together with unbelievers: for what fellowship hath righteousness with unrighteousness? and what communion hath light with darkness? (2 Corinthians 6:14)

Then said the LORD unto me, Go yet, love a woman beloved of her friend, yet an adulteress, according to the love of the LORD toward the children of Israel, who look to other gods, and love flagons of wine. So I bought her to me for fifteen pieces of silver, and for an ho'-mer of barley, and an half ho'-mer of barley (Hosea 3:1-2).

CONFESSION

According to Webster's New Compact Dictionary, to confess is to acknowledge or disclose one's misdeed, fault, or sin(s). Sin separates us from God; it also hinders our spiritual growth and effectiveness in the body of Christ. Therefore, we must make confessions of our sins unto God.

Confession is simply acknowledging and admitting to God that at some point, we have rejected his Word. In order for God to forgive our sins, we must first confess them. Our confessions must be sincere and directly from our hearts; God knows all things.

Confess your faults one to another, and pray one for another, that ye may be healed. The effectual fervent prayer of a righteous man availeth much (James 5:16).

And it shall be, when he shall be guilty in one of these things, that he shall confess that he hath sinned in that thing (Leviticus 5:5).

If they shall confess their iniquity, and the iniquity of their fathers, with their trespass which they trespassed against me, and that also they have walked contrary unto me (Leviticus 26:40).

Howbeit thou art just in all that is brought upon us; for thou hast done right, but we have done wickedly: Neither have our kings, our princes, our priests, nor our fathers, kept thy law, nor hearkened unto thy commandments and thy testimonies, wherewith thou didst testify against them (Nehemiah 9:33-34).

And said, O my God, I am ashamed and blush to lift up my face to thee, my God: for our iniquities are increased over our head, and our trespass is grown up unto the heavens (Ezra 9:6).

And Joshua said unto A'-chan, My son, give, I pray thee, glory to the LORD God of Israel, and make confession unto him; and tell me now what thou hast done; hide it not from me (Joshua 7:19).

And after all that is come upon us for our evil deeds, and for our great trespass, seeing that thou our God hast punished us less than our iniquities deserve, and hast given us such deliverance as this (Ezra 9:13)

Only acknowledge thine iniquity, that thou hast transgressed against the LORD thy God, and hast scattered thy ways to the strangers under every green tree, and ye have not obeyed my voice, saith the LORD (Jeremiah 3:13).

He that covereth his sins shall not prosper: but whoso confesseth and forsaketh them shall have mercy (Proverbs 28:13).

I have sinned; what Shall I do unto thee, O thou preserver of men? Why hast thou set me as a mark against thee, so that I am a burden to myself? (Job 7:20).

REPENTANCE

Repentance usually occurs when one recognizes that he or she is under condemnation of God's law. It is performed to acquire a changed mind, forsake one's sins, and seek God's forgiveness. Repentance is growth toward God which enables us to receive his fulfilled promises.

For I have no pleasure in the death of him that dieth, saith the Lord God: wherefore turn yourselves, and live ye (Ezekiel 18:32).

Or despisest thou the riches of his goodness and forbearance and longsuffering; not knowing that the goodness of God leadeth thee to repentance? (Romans 2:4)

Repent ye therefore, and be converted, that your sins may be blotted out, when the times of refreshing shall come from the presence of the LORD (Acts 3:19).

But if we walk in the light, as he is in the light, we have fellowship one with another, and the blood of Jesus Christ his Son cleanseth us from all sin (1 John 1:7).

Draw nigh to God, and he will draw nigh to you. Cleanse your hands, ye sinners; and purify your hearts, ye double minded (James 4:8).

And ye have forgotten the exhortation which speaketh unto you as unto children, My son, despise not thou the chastening of the Lord, nor faint when thou art rebuked of him (Hebrews 12:5).

And be not conformed to this world: but be ye transformed by the renewing of your mind, that ye may prove what is that good, and acceptable, and perfect, will of God (Romans 12:2).

Stand in awe, and sin not: commune with your own heart upon your bed, and be still. Selah (Psalm 4:4).

And saying, Repent ye: for the kingdom of heaven is at hand (Matthew 3:2).

Repent therefore of this thy wickedness, and pray God, if perhaps the thought of thine heart may be forgiven thee (Acts 8:22).

I tell you, Nay: but, except ye repent, ye shall all likewise perish (Luke 13:3).

I say unto you, that likewise joy shall be in heaven over one sinner that repenteth, more than over ninety and nine just persons, which need no repentance (Luke 15:7).

SELF-FORGIVENESS

According to *Webster's New Compact Dictionary,* to forgive is to pardon; to give up resentment of; to cease to feel resentment against.

God has forgiven you from the very moment that you asked for his forgiveness. You must learn to discontinue judging yourself for your past mistakes. Notice that the key word utilized in the sentence is "past." According to Webster's New Compact Dictionary, the past is referred to as having to do with or existing at a former time, before the present time; a person's history or background that therefore has no affiliation with a person's future. Jesus is willing to pardon each of our sins—no matter how great—but he instructs us not to be repeat offenders of sin.

And the scribes and Pharisees brought unto him a woman taken in adultery; and when they had set her in the midst, They say unto him, Master, this woman was taken in adultery, in the very act. Now Moses in the law commanded us, that such should be stoned: but what sayest thou? This they said, tempting him, that they might have to accuse him. But Jesus stooped down, and with his finger wrote on the ground, as though he heard them not. So when they continued asking him, he lifted up himself, and said unto them, He that is without sin among you, let him first cast a stone at her. And again he stooped down, and wrote on the ground. And they which heard it, being convicted by their own conscience, went out one by one, beginning at the eldest, even unto the last: and Jesus was left alone, and the woman standing in the midst. When Jesus had lifted up himself, and saw none but the woman, he said unto her, Woman, where are those thine accusers?

Hath no man condemned thee? She said, No man, Lord. And Jesus said unto her, Neither do I condemn thee: go, and sin no more (John 8:3-11).

And shewing mercy unto thousands of them that love me, and keep my commandments (Exodus 20:6).

Chapter Five

JEALOUSY

Ye shall not go after other gods, of the gods of the people which are round about you;(Deuteronomy 6:14).

God is a jealous God with a righteous jealousy. God's jealousy is a result of his unconditional love for his children and his desire for us to have the very best in Christ Jesus. Anything that removes our focus away from God is considered to be detrimental to our relationship with him. In fact, the very idea of God's children worshipping other idols is odious to him. Idols can consist of almost anything—for example: a spouse, children, a career, cars, homes, etc. God will not allow any relationship to prosper that will interfere with our dedicated relationship to him.

(For the LORD thy God is a jealous God among you) lest the anger of the LORD thy God be kindled against thee, and destroy thee from off the face of the earth (Deuteronomy 6:15).

For the LORD thy God is a consuming fire, even a jealous God (Deuteronomy 4:24).

Thus saith the LORD of hosts; I was jealous for Zion with great jealousy, and I was jealous for her with great fury (Zechariah 8:2).

Thou shalt not bow down thyself to them, nor serve them: for I the LORD thy God am a jealous God, visiting the iniquity of the fathers upon the children unto the third and fourth generation of them that hate me (Exodus 20:5).

Do we provoke the Lord to jealousy? are we stronger than he? (1 Corinthians 10:22)

Now that you have knowledge of the truth, you must obey. Please forsake your ungodly ways to prevent willful sin.

For if we sin wilfully after that we have received the knowledge of the truth, there remaineth no more sacrifices for sins (Hebrews 10:26).

A WOMAN'S JEALOUSY AND ENVY

A jealous woman seeks to discredit, criticize, and destroy the character of another woman. Insecurity is responsible for her lack of confidence within herself, so in an effort to fulfill the void within her, she lashes out against others who have what she lacks.

I believe that many parents are responsible for the monstrous attitudes that they created within their daughters by failing to teach them to truly *love* themselves. The reality is that regardless to how beautiful you are, there's someone whose beauty exceeds yours, and no matter how wealthy you are, there's always someone who is much wealthier. Jealousy expresses one's desperate desire to achieve something lacked, and the more difficult it becomes to achieve the goal, the more intense the jealously becomes. Jealousy can become so intense that it can no longer be hidden.

You can spend your entire life being jealous of others, or you can focus on loving others—the choice is yours. In order for a jealous woman to conquer the spirit of jealousy, she must first embrace the woman that God created her to be and realize that she doesn't need to change who she is in order to become like someone else. No one can possibly be beautiful if they're ashamed of their self-image.

Jealousy is simply thinking someone else has something that you desire but don't or can't have. Instead of being jealous, one should practice admiring another woman's strength and attributes. In addition, stop comparing yourself to other women. God has created you unique—a limited edition—so *love* yourself, and refuse to allow years to go by without really having a relationship with yourself.

Again, *love* the woman that God has designed you to be. You will be amazed at the qualities you possess but never took the time to recognize. Always be thankful to God for the gifts he's blessed others with. If you're truly sincere about your happiness for someone else, God will bless you with just as much—if not more—in your season. Recognize that when God is blessing someone, it is because it is his or her season, and your season is on the way if you continue to hold on to God's promises.

GOD does all things by seasons. You must learn to be grateful for the wonderful gifts that God has given you thus far and begin focusing on all of the positive aspects of your life. You must renew your mind by thinking positively toward others.

A sound heart is the life of the flesh: but envy the rottenness of the bones (Proverbs 14:30).

But if you have bitter envying and strife in your hearts, glory not, and lie not against the truth . . . For where envying and strife is, there is confusion and every evil work (James 3:14, 16).

Be not overcome of evil, but overcome evil with good (Romans 12:21).

Wrath is cruel, and anger is outrageous; but who is able to stand before envy? (Proverbs 27:4)

From whence come wars and fightings among you? come they not hence, even of your lusts that war in your members? Ye lust, and have not: ye kill, and desire to have, and cannot obtain: ye fight and war, yet ye have not, because ye ask not. Ye ask, and receive not, because ye ask amiss, that ye may consume it upon your lusts (James 4:1-3).

For ye are yet carnal: for whereas there is among you envying, and strife, and divisions, are ye not carnal, and walk as men? (1 Corinthians 3:3)

THE DIFFERENCE

God's jealousy for humanity differs from the jealousy of mankind. God's jealousy is related to our worship of idols or anything that separates us from his unconditional love. The jealousy of mankind consists of passionate jealousy or envy of material possessions. God doesn't envy mankind for material possessions, and although he hates sin, he doesn't hate the sinner—after all, he created us in his image.

The earth is the LORD'S, and the fullness thereof; the world, and they that dwell therein (Psalm 24:1).

In the beginning God created the heaven and the earth . . . So God created man in his own image, in the image of God created he him; male and female created he them . . . And God saw everything that he had made, and, behold, it was very good. And the evening and the morning were the sixth day (Genesis 1:1, 27, 31).

Chapter Six

LOVING YOUR CHILDREN

Those who are parents must love their children without any limitations or expectations. You must rear them in a safe, stable home, surrounded by lots of love, joy, laughter, hugs, and kisses. Each moment of your life should present another opportunity to express your love for them via words and deeds. Whenever your family members are away from each other for any purpose (school, work, etc.), you must reassure your children of how much you have missed them.

Encourage your children to do their very best in all of their endeavors, and inspire them never to quit, because a winner will never quit, and a quitter will never win. When your children accomplish anything—small or great—you must praise them for their achievements, as this encourages them to continue to strive for the best.

Teaching your children manners is highly important; therefore, you should always practice being polite and thanking them whenever they assist you with anything or say anything nice. In spite of anything that you can possibly give to your children, your love for them supersedes all.

He maketh the barren woman to keep house, and to be a joyful mother of children. Praise ye the LORD (Psalm 113:9).

Lo, children are an heritage of the LORD: and the fruit of the womb is his reward. As arrows are in the hand of a mighty man; so are children of the youth. Happy is the man that hath his quiver full of them: they shall not be ashamed, but they shall speak with the enemies in the gate (Psalm 127:3-5).

Children's children are the crown of old men; and the glory of children are their fathers (Proverbs 17:6).

And he lifted up his eyes, and saw the women and the children; and said, Who are those with thee? And he said, The children which God hath graciously given thy servant (Genesis 33:5).

Take heed that ye despise not one of these little ones; for I say unto you, That in heaven their angels do always behold the face of my Father which is in heaven (Matthew 18:10).

ILLUSTRATIONS OF A PARENT'S LOVE

Then came there two women, that were harlots, unto the king, and stood before him. And the one woman said O my lord, I and this woman dwell in one house; and I was delivered of a child with her in the house. And it came to pass the third day after that I was delivered, that this woman was delivered also: and we were together; there was no stranger with us in the house, save we two in the house. And this woman's child died in the night; because she overlaid it. And she arose at midnight, and took my son from beside me, while thine handmaid slept, and laid it in her bosom, and laid her dead child in my bosom. And when I rose in the morning to give my child suck, behold, it was dead: but when I had considered it in the morning, behold, it was not my son, which I did bear. And the other woman said, Nay; but the living is my son, and the dead is thy son. And this said, No; but the dead is thy son, and the living is my son. Thus they spake before the king. Then said the king, The one saith, This is my son that liveth, and thy son is the dead: and the other saith, Nay; but thy son is the dead, and my son is the living. And the king said, Bring me a sword. And they brought a sword before the king. And the king said, Divide the living child in two, and give half to the one, and half to the other. Then spake the woman whose the living child was unto the king, for her bowels yearned upon her son, and she said, O my lord, give her the living child, and in no wise slay it. But the other said, Let it be neither mine nor thine, but divide it. Then the king answered and said, Give her the living child, and in no wise slay it: She is the mother thereof. (1 Kings 3:16-27)

The love of the mother of the living child was demonstrated by her willingness to allow the mother of the overlaid child to have her living child to raise as her own in effort to prevent harm upon him.

NO GREATER LOVE

For God so loved the world, that he gave his only begotten Son, that whosoever believeth in him shall not perish, but have everlasting life. For God sent not his Son into the world to condemn the world; but that the world through him might be saved (John 3:16-17).

Greater love hath no man than this, that a man lay down his life for his friends (John 15:13).

God's love for his children (humanity) was demonstrated when he sent his Son to die for the sins of mankind.

INTRODUCING YOUR CHILDREN TO THE LORD

You must introduce your children to the Lord while they are still in the womb. How is this possible? Through the power of prayer, biblical literature, and regular church services, your unborn child can be introduced to the Lord. As children are in their growing years, you can continue to take them to church services regularly.

The introduction of prayer is another tool that can be utilized in your mission to help your children establish an inseparable bond with Jesus. All parents are responsible for introducing their children to the Lord. Parents are also accountable for the behavior they display in the presence of their children, because your children are searching for Christ within you—not in words only, but also in deeds.

Not forsaking the assembling of ourselves together, as the manner of some is; but exhorting one another: and so much the more, as ye see the day approaching (Hebrews 10:25).

And ye shall teach them your children, speaking of them when thou sittest in thine house, and when thou walkest by the way, when thou liest down, and when thou risest up. And thou shalt write them upon the door posts of thine house, and upon thy gates: That your days may be multiplied, and the days of your children, in the land which the LORD sware unto your fathers to give them, as the days of heaven upon the earth. For if ye shall diligently keep all these commandments which I command you, to do them, to love the LORD your God, to walk in all his ways, and to cleave unto him (Deuteronomy 11:19-22)

Only take heed to thyself, and keep thy soul diligently, lest thou forget the things which thine eyes have seen, and lest they depart from thy heart all the days of thy life: but teach them thy sons, and thy sons' sons; (Deuteronomy 4:9).

Gather the people together, men, and women, and children, and thy stranger that is within thy gates, that they may hear, and that they may learn, and fear the LORD your God, and observe to do all the words of this law: And that their children, which have not known any thing, may hear, and learn to fear the LORD your God, as long as ye live in the land whither ye go over Jordan to possess it. (Deuteronomy 31:12-13)

And it shall come to pass, when all these things are come upon thee, the blessing and the curse, which I have set before thee, and thou shalt call them to mind among all the nations, whither the LORD thy God hath driven thee, And shalt return unto the LORD thy God, and shalt obey his voice according to all that I commanded thee this day, thou and thy children, with all thine heart, and with all thy soul; That then the LORD thy God will turn thy captivity, and have compassion upon thee, and will return and gather thee from all the nations, whither the LORD thy God hath scattered thee (Deuteronomy 30:1-3).

Ye shall fear every man his mother, and his father, and keep my sabbaths: I am the LORD your God (Leviticus 19:3).

But I said unto their children in the wilderness, Walk ye not in the statues of your fathers, neither observe their judgments, nor defile yourselves with their idols (Ezekiel 20:18).

And when the chief priests and scribes saw the wonderful things that he did, and the children crying in the temple, and saying, Ho-san'-na to the son of David; they were sore displeased, And said unto him, Hearest thou what these say? And Jesus saith unto them, Yea; have ye never read, Out of the mouth of babes and sucklings thou hast perfected praise? (Matthew 21:15-16).

My son, fear thou the LORD and the king: and meddle not with them that are given to change (Proverbs 24:21).

DISCIPLINING YOUR CHILDREN

All children must be subject to some form of discipline for their misbehaviors. Most of the time, it's difficult for mothers to tolerate the child being disciplined by the father, so she intervenes in an attempt to protect the child but only stirs up strife between her husband and herself. This doesn't necessarily indicate that she's a bad mother but that she simply used poor judgment.

A mother's decision to intervene when her child is being disciplined is a natural instinct, as mothers are protectors of their children by nature. However, her actions encourage a child to respect one parent but not the other. Children prey on the weakness of their parents. Therefore, if your husband places the child on restrictions as a form discipline, you must enforce the restrictions. Fathers are usually very firm with their children and are the disciplinarians in the home.

In an effort to deescalate problems, I suggest that you stand firmly behind your husband's decisions where your children are concerned. Mothers are usually more lenient than necessary, and because of their lack of discipline, unfortunately, some children have gone astray. You must never allow your children to observe any disagreements between you and your spouse that concern them. However, if you have any issues or concerns, please express them to your spouse whenever the two of you are alone. Children will manipulate one parent against the other if given the chance to do so. You and your spouse must always display unity where your children are concerned.

God didn't instruct us to allow our children to make their own decisions in order to remain friends with them. It isn't possible to raise a child effectively if you are attempting to be his or her friend. Don't get any misconceptions; we must establish a friendship with our children to ensure them that they can rely upon us to protect them. However, we mustn't allow our friendship to affect our ability to use proper judgment when making decisions for our children or to discipline when necessary.

When necessary, you must allow your husband to discipline your children at his discretion, without interfering, as long as the children aren't being abused. Again, if you have any concerns, you must express them when the two of you are alone. In conclusion, please strive to be of one accord with your spouse in raising your children.

Can two walk together, except they be agreed? (Amos 3:3)

He that spareth his rod hateth his son: but he that loveth him chasteneth him betimes (Proverbs 13:24).

And ye have forgotten the exhortation which speaketh unto you as unto children, My son, despise not thou the chastening of the Lord, nor faint when thou art rebuked of him . . . Now no chastening for the present seemeth to be joyous, but grievous: nevertheless afterward it yieldeth the peaceable fruit of righteousness unto them which are excercised thereby (Hebrews 12:5,11).

Children, obey your parents in the Lord: for this is right. Honour thy father and mother; which is the first commandment with promise; That it may be well with thee, and thou mayest live long on the earth (Ephesians 6:1-3).

Honour thy father and thy mother, as the LORD thy God hath commanded thee; that thy days may be prolonged, and that it may go well with thee, in the land which the LORD thy God giveth thee. (Deuteronomy 5:16)

If a man have a stubborn and rebellious son, which will not obey the voice of his father, or the voice of his mother, and that, when they have chasteneth him, will not hearken unto them: Then Shall his father and his mother lay hold on him, and bring him out unto the elders of his city, and unto the gate of his place; And they shall say unto the elders of his city, This our son is stubborn and rebellious, he will not obey our voice; he is glutton, and a drunkard. And all the men of his city shall stone him with stones, that he die: so shalt thou put evil away from among you; and all Israel shall hear, and fear (Deuteronomy 21:18-21).

My son, keep thy father's commandment, and forsake not the law of thy mother . . . For the commandment is a lamp; and the law is light; and reproofs of instruction are the way of life (Proverbs 6:20, 23).

He is in the way of life that keepeth instruction: but he that refuseth reproof erreth (Proverbs 10:17).

Train up a child in the way he should go: and when he is old, he will not depart from it . . . Foolishness is bound in the heart of a child; but the rod of correction shall drive it far from him (Proverbs 22:6, 15).

Chasten thy son while there is hope, and let not thy soul spare for his crying (Proverbs 19:18).

The rod and reproof give wisdom: but a child left to himself bringeth his mother to shame . . . Correct thy son, and he shall give thee rest; yea, he shall give delight unto thy soul (Proverbs 29:15, 17).

A fool despiseth his father's instruction: but he that regardeth reproof is prudent . . . He that refuseth instruction despiseth his own soul: but he that heareth reproof getteth understanding (Proverbs 15:5, 32).

RESPECTER OF PERSONS AMONG YOUR CHILDREN

Having respecter of persons is showing partiality.

I'm disgusted by parents who have respecter of persons among their children. Your children never asked to be born, and it's very unfortunate for them when they are being mistreated for reasons that are beyond their control. A child should never be made to feel inferior to a sibling by his or her parent or parents. Although one of your children may meet all of your expectations while the other doesn't meet any, the fact is that they are all your children.

I simply can't digest how a mother could purposely love one child more than the other when she carried them both in her womb and travailed with them both. I suppose a mother's decision to treat her children differently is often associated with her feelings toward the child's father in situations where the children have different fathers. But nonetheless, the children only have one mother, who they should be able to depend upon to treat them fairly.

A mother loves her children no matter what has transpired or will transpire in her relationships with their fathers. Mothers, you carried and nourished your children inside of your womb. They were attached to your umbilical cord, and though the cord was physically cut after their birth, there should never be a spiritual separation. Love all of your children equally, and if for any reason you find it difficult to do so, you must seek God in prayer immediately.

There are many consequences when favortisim is displayed among siblings. For example, favoritism is one of the leading causes of hate and strife between siblings today. Would you like to be held accountable to God for the separation of your children? More often than not, the child that you have loved the most will neglect you in later years, while the child you neglected will be the one to provide care for you.

Now Israel loved Joseph more than all his children, because he was the son of his old age: and he made him a coat of many colours. And when his brethren saw that their father loved him more than all his brethren, they hated him, and could not speak peaceably unto him (Genesis 37:3-4).

For there is no respect of persons with God (Romans 2:11).

And if ye call on the Father, who without respect of persons judgeth according to every man's work, pass the time of your sojourning here in fear (1 Peter 1:17).

My brethren, have not the faith of our Lord Jesus Christ, the Lord of glory, with respect of persons. For if there come unto your assembly a man with a gold ring, in goodly apparel, and there come in also a poor man in vile raiment; And ye have respect to him that weareth the gay clothing, and say unto him, Sit thou here in a good place; and say to the poor, Stand thou there, or sit here under my footstool: Are ye not then partial in yourselves, and are become judges of evil thoughts? (James 2:1-4).

But he that doeth wrong shall receive for the wrong which he hath done: and there is no respect of persons (Colossians 3:25).

Knowing that whatsoever good thing any man doeth, the same shall he receive of the Lord, whether he be bond or free. And, ye masters, do the same things unto them, forbearing threatening: knowing that your Master also is in heaven; neither is there respect of persons with him (Ephesians 6:8-9).

WHAT IS THE CHURCH?

The church is a building where worship and praise to the almighty God is conducted. It is also considered to be the dressing room in which we prepare for heaven.

WHAT IS THE PURPOSE OF THE CHURCH?

The church is a place for emotional, physical, and spiritual healing. It is a bridge of hope to those who are lost and wishing to establish or restore their relationship with Jesus Christ. The church is a place for profound biblical teachings, worship, and praise!

And, having made peace through the blood of his cross, by him to reconcile all things unto himself; by him, I say, whether they be things in earth, or things in heaven (Colossians 1:20).

For as the body is one, and hath many members, and all the members of that one body, being many, are one body: so also is Christ. For by one spirit are we all baptized into one body, whether we be Jews or Gentiles, whether we be bond or free; and have been all made to drink into one Spirit. For the body is not one member, but many . . . But now hath God set the members every one of them in the body, as it hath pleased him (1 Corinthians 12:12-14, 18).

Then they that gladly received his word were baptized: and the same day there were added unto them about three thousand souls (Acts 2:41).

Is any sick among you? let him call for the elders of the church; and let them pray over him, anointing him with oil in the name of the Lord (James 5:14).

And they cast out many devils, and anointed with oil many that were sick, and healed them (Mark 6:13).

The Spirit of the Lord is upon me, because he hath anointed me to preach the gospel to the poor; he hath sent me to heal the brokenhearted, to preach deliverance to the captives, and recovering of sight to the blind, to set at liberty them that are bruised, To preach the acceptable year of the Lord (Luke 4:18-19).

And he is the head of the body, the church: who is the beginning, the firstborn from the dead; that in all things he might have the preeminence (Colossians 1:18).

For both he that sanctifieth and they who are sanctified are all of one: for which cause he is not ashamed to call them brethren. Saying, I will declare thy name unto my brethren, in the midst of the church will I sing praise unto thee (Hebrews 2:11-12).

And let us consider one another to provoke unto love and to good works: Not forsaking the assembling of ourselves together, as the manner of some is; but exhorting one another: and so much the more, as ye see the day approaching (Hebrews 10:24-25).

And in very deed for this cause have I raised thee up, for to shew in thee my power; and that my name may be declared throughout all the earth (Exodus 9:16).

ARE WE REQUIRED TO TITHE?

The Lord didn't suggest or ask that we tithe but commanded that we tithe.

Bring ye all the tithes into the storehouse, that there may be meat in mine house, and prove me now herewith, saith the LORD of hosts, if I will not open you the windows of heaven, and pour you out a blessing, that there shall not be room enough to receive it (Malachi 3:10).

HOW MUCH OF MY INCOME MUST I TITHE?

God requires a tenth (10 percent) of our income, although you may give more (but certainly not any less).

And this stone, which I have set for a pillar, shall be God's house: and of all that thou shalt give me I will surely give the tenth unto thee (Genesis 28:22).

WHERE MUST I SUBMIT MY TITHES?

Malachi 3:10 instructs us to bring our tithes into the storehouse, which in modern times is the church.

ARE THERE ANY BENEFITS TO TITHING?

There are always benefits in obeying the voice of the Lord.

And I will rebuke the devourer for your sakes, and he shall not destroy the fruits of your ground; neither shall your vine cast her fruit before the time in the field, saith the LORD of hosts (Malachi 3:11).

WHAT IF I TITHE TO BE OBEDIENT TO GOD BUT REALLY DON'T WANT TO?

God doesn't want us to give grudgingly.

Every man according as he purposeth in his heart, so let him give; not grudgingly, or of necessity: for God loveth a cheerful giver (2 Corinthians 9:7).

WHAT IF MY PASTOR IS MISHANDLING THE MONEY FOR PERSONAL USE?

God has commanded us to "bring ye all tithes into the storehouse (Malachi 3:10)," and when you have done that, you have obeyed God. All he expects from us is obedience, and everything else is in his hands. Although he is aware that some pastors will be dishonest, God never commanded us to worry about how our tithes are spent.

God isn't the author of confusion but a God of order. God didn't give any sheep (laborers in the gospel) the authority to correct his shepherds (pastors); therefore, if the pastor is guilty of misusing God's money, then the pastor will be held accountable for poor stewardship. Don't gossip about your pastor even if you feel that he's done wrong.

I advise you to pray concerning any issues that you may be experiencing with the church, and if God directs you to depart the church, please do so peacefully. Speaking against your pastor wouldn't resolve the issues, as this is a matter that only God can resolve. I also forewarn you not to put your mouth on (to speak negatively about) God's anointed ones (men and women of God), as your mouth will cause your flesh to suffer (curses will fall upon you). Therefore, if you're planning to depart the church, I suggest that you do so with the blessings of God and your pastors instead of departing with a curse.

And Miriam and Aaron spake against Moses because of the E-thi-o'-pi-an woman whom he had married: for he had married an E-thi-o'-pi-an woman. And they said, Hath the LORD indeed spoken only by Moses? Hath he not spoken also by us? And the LORD heard it. (Now the man Moses was very meek, above all the men which were upon the face of the earth.) And the LORD spake suddenly unto Moses, and unto Aaron, and unto Miriam, Come out ye three unto the tabernacle of the congregation. And they three came out. And the LORD came down in the pillar of the cloud, and stood in the door of the tabernacle, and called Aaron and Miriam: and they both came forth. And he said, Hear now my words: If there be a prophet among you, I the LORD will make myself known unto him in a vision, and will speak unto him in a dream. My servant Moses is not so, who is faithful in all mine house. With him will I speak mouth to mouth, even apparently, and not in dark speeches; and the similitude of the LORD shall he behold: wherefore then were ye not afraid to speak against my servant Moses? And the anger of the LORD was kindled against them; and he departed. And the cloud departed from off the tabernacle; and, behold, Miriam became leprous, white as snow: and Aaron looked upon Miriam, and, behold, she was leprous. And Aaron said unto Moses, Alas, my lord, I beseech thee, lay not the sin upon us, wherein we have done foolishly, and wherein we have sinned (Numbers 12:1-11).

Thou shalt truly tithe all the increase of thy seed, that the field bringeth forth year by year (Deuteronomy 14:22).

Burning lips and a wicked heart are like a potsherd covered with silver dross (Proverbs 26:23).

Saying, Touch not mine anointed, and do my prophets no harm (Psalm 105:15).

For God is not the author of confusion, but of peace, as in all churches of the saints (1 Corinthians 14:33).

A false witness shall not be unpunished, and he that speaketh lies shall perish (Proverbs 19:9).

Suffer not thy mouth to cause thy flesh to sin; neither say thou before the angel, that it was an error: wherefore should God be angry at thy voice, and destroy the work of thine hands? (Ecclesiastes 5:6)

HYPOCRITES

For such are false apostles, deceitful workers, transforming themselves into the apostles of Christ. And no marvel; for Satan himself is transformed into an angel of light (2 Corinthians 11:13-14).

As the Sadducees and Pharisees were hypocrites in Jesus's day, so are many, many folks today. Most of them believe that God exists but doubt his power. Under pretense, they go into the church in the presence of others. They praise God, speak in unknown tongues, and worship. They serve God externally, but their hearts are very distant from the truth.

This kind shouldn't be referred to as Christians but as religious folks, because they attend church services religiously, yet they don't have a sincere relationship or connection with God. They pretend to be plugged in to the source (God) when the truth is that they never knew him. These people possess the spirits of backbiting, lying, false accusation, and whoredom and are busybodies.

It's irrelevant to state that hypocrites' hearts were turned from God when their hearts were never turned toward him. They are recognized as seducing spirits, and they're on a mission to destroy the body of Christ. They have taken the form of holy men and women of God. This is why we must know those who labor among us in the gospel.

There are also those who once believed but were lured away by demonic forces through the lusts of their flesh. These are recognized as apostates (ones who forsake their faith), because they were lured away from the truth by false religion and practices which are contrary to the Word of God. As angels have fallen from heaven, so have they fallen from the faith (2 Peter 2:4). They are condemned and are seeking to condemn others. Be prayerful and watchful of this kind.

Ye blind guides, which strain at a gnat, and swallow a camel. Woe unto you, scribes and Pharisees, hypocrites! For ye make clean the outside of the cup and of the platter, but within they are full of extortion and excess. Thou blind Pharisee, cleanse first that which is within the cup and platter, that the outside of them may be clean also (Matthew 23:24-26).

In this the children of God are manifest, and the children of the devil: whosoever doeth not righteousness is not of God, neither he that loveth not his brother (1 John 3:10).

I will send him against an hypocritical nation, and against the people of my wrath will I give him a charge, to take the spoil, and to take the prey, and to tread them down like the mire of the streets (Isaiah 10:6).

Now therefore know certainly that ye shall die by the sword, by the famine, and by the pestilence, in the place whither ye desire to go and to sojourn (Jeremiah 42:22).

Because ye have said, We have made a covenant with death, and with hell are we at agreement; when the overflowing scourge shall pass through, it shall not come unto us: for we have made lies our refuge, and under falsehood have we hid ourselves (Isaiah 28:15).

Woe unto you, scribes and Pharisees, hypocrites! For ye pay tithe of mint and anise and cummin, and have omitted the weightier matters of the law, judgment, mercy, and faith: these ought ye to have done, and not to leave the other undone . . . Woe unto you, scribes and Pharisees, hypocrites! For ye are like unto whited sepulchres, which indeed appear beautiful outward, but are within full of dead men's bones, and of all uncleanness. Even so ye also outwardly appear righteous unto men, but within ye are full of hypocrisy and iniquity. Woe unto you, scribes and Pharisees, hypocrites! Because ye build the tombs of the prophets, and garnish the sepulchres of the righteous . . . Ye serpents, ye generation of vipers, how can you escape the damnation of hell? (Matthew 23:23, 27-29, 33)

For, lo, they that are far from thee shall perish: thou hast destroyed all them that go a whoring from thee (Psalm 73:27).

And we beseech you, brethren, to know them which labour among you, and are over you in the Lord, and admonish you (1 Thessalonians 5:12).

Beloved, believe not every spirit, but try the spirits whether they are of God: because many false prophets are gone out into the world (1 John 4:1).

But the end of all things is at hand: be ye therefore sober, and watch unto prayer (1 Peter 4:7).

I am the good shepherd, and know my sheep, and am known of mine (John 10:14).

WHAT IS THE ANOINTING OF GOD?

The anointing of God is the burden-removing, yoke-destroying *power of God.*

And it shall come to pass in that day, that his burden shall be taken away from off thy shoulder, and his yoke from off thy neck, and the yolk shall be destroyed because of the anointing (Isaiah 10:27).

The anointing is the divine power that God gives to those he has appointed to execute his purposes. The work of God cannot be performed through natural human power but by his Holy Spirit. The anointing works internally and externally through those God has appointed. The anointing works internally to conform us to the likeness of God and externally for the manifestation of Jesus Christ through healings, preaching, teaching, witnessing, etc.

Although there are many callings in the body of Christ, there's only one purpose. Each believer has a different calling and is anointed and equipped according to his purpose.

The Spirit of the LORD God is upon me, because the LORD hath anointed me to preach good tidings unto the meek; he hath sent me to bind up the brokenhearted, to proclaim liberty to the captives, and the opening of the prison to them that are bound (Isaiah 61:1).

Thou hast loved righteousness, and hated iniquity; therefore God, even thy God, hath anointed thee with the oil of gladness above thy fellows (Hebrews 1:9).

Now he which stablisheth us with you in Christ, and hath anointed us, is God (2 Corinthians 1:21).

But the anointing which ye have received of him abideth in you, and ye need not that any man teach you: but as the same anointing teacheth you of all things, and is truth, and is no lie, and even as it hath taught you, ye shall abide in him (1 John 2:27).

I have found David my servant; with my holy oil have I anointed him (Psalm 89:20).

Now know I that the LORD saveth his anointed; he will hear him from his holy heaven with the saving strength of his right hand (Psalm 20:6).

Great deliverance giveth he to his king; and sheweth mercy to his anointed, to David, and to his seed for evermore (Psalm 18:50).

HOW CAN I LOSE MY ANOINTING?

Anointing comes from the presence of God in our lives. Sin separates us from God; therefore, when we neglect his Word, God's holy presence departs from us. Disobedience is the primary reason the anointing departs a believer's life. When we yield to the lusts of the flesh, the enemy—our secret assassin—is enabled to gain entry into our lives to destroy them.

The thief cometh not, but for to steal, and to kill, and to destroy: I am come that they might have life, and that they might have it more abundantly (John 10:10).

Now go and smite Am'-a-lek, and utterly destroy all that they have, and spare them not; but slay both man and woman, infant and suckling, ox and sheep, camel and ass. And Saul gathered the people together, and numbered them in Te-la'-im, two hundred thousand footmen, and ten thousand men of Judah. And Saul came to a city of Am'-a-lek, and laid wait in the valley. And Saul said unto the Ken'-ites, Go, depart, get you down from among the Am'-a-lek-ites, lest I destroy you with them: for ye shewed kindness to all the children of Israel, when they came up out of Egypt. So the Ken'-ites departed from among the Am'-a-lek-ites. And Saul smote the Am'-a-lek-ites from Hav'-i-lah until thou comest to Shur, that is over against Egypt. And he took A'-gag the king of the Am'-a-lek-ites alive, and utterly destroyed all the people with the edge of the sword. But Saul and the people spared A'-gag, and the best of the sheep, and of the oxen, and of the fatlings, and the lambs, and all that was good, and would not utterly destroy them: but every thing that was vile and refuse, that they destroyed utterly. Then came the word of the LORD unto Samuel, saying, It repenteth me that I have set up Saul to be king: for he is turned back from following me, and hath not performed my commandments. And it grieved Samuel; and he cried unto the LORD all night. And when Samuel rose early to meet Saul in the morning, it was told Samuel, saying, Saul came to Carmel, and behold, he set up a place, and is gone about, and passed on, and gone down to Gil'-gal. And Samuel came to Saul: and Saul said unto him, Blessed be thou of the LORD: I have performed the commandment of the LORD. And Samuel said, What meaneth then this bleating of the sheep in mine ears, and the lowing of the oxen which I hear? And Saul said, They have brought them from the Am'-a-lek-ites: for the people spared the best of the sheep and of the oxen, to sacrifice unto the LORD thy God; and the rest we have utterly destroyed. Then Samuel said to Saul, Stay, and I will tell thee what the LORD hath said to me this night. And he said unto him, Say on. And Samuel said, When thou wast little in thine own sight, wast thou not made the head of the tribes of Israel, and the LORD anointed thee king over Israel? And the LORD sent thee on a journey, and said, Go and utterly destroy the sinners the Am'-a-lek-ites, and fight against them until they be consumed. Wherefore then didst thou not obey the voice of the LORD, but didst fly upon the spoil, and didst evil in the sight of the LORD? And Saul said unto Samuel, Yea, I have obeyed the voice of the LORD, and have gone the way which the LORD sent me, and have brought A'gag the king of Am'-a-lek, and have utterly destroyed the Am'a-lek-ites. But the people took of the spoil, sheep and oxen, the chief of the things which should have been utterly destroyed, to sacrifice unto the LORD thy God in Gil'-gal. And Samuel said, Hath the LORD as great delight in burnt offerings and sacrifices, as in obeying the voice of the LORD? Behold, to obey is better than sacrifice, and to hearken than the fat of rams. For rebellion is as the sin of witchcraft, and stubbornness is as iniquity and idolatry. Because thou hast rejected the word of the LORD, he hath also rejected thee from being king. And Saul said unto Samuel, I have sinned: for I have transgressed the commandment of the LORD, and thy words: because I have feared the people, and obeyed their voice. Now therefore, I pray thee, pardon my sin, and turn again with me, that I may worship the LORD. And Samuel said unto Saul, I will not return with thee: for thou hast rejected the word of the LORD, and the LORD hath rejected thee from being king over Israel. And as Samuel turned about to go away, he laid hold upon the skirt of his mantle, and it rent. And Samuel said unto him, The LORD hath rent the kingdom of Israel from thee this day, and hath given it to a neighbor of thine, that is better than thou. And also the Strength of Israel will not lie nor repent: for he is not a man, that he should repent (1 Samuel 15:3-29).

PROTECTING YOUR ANOINTING

Anointing is a supernatural, precious, priceless, timeless gift that only God can give. It is an irreplaceable gift that you must always treasure. You must never allow yourself to be placed in a situation that will compromise your anointing. You must always protect your anointing as a loving mother protects her newborn child. By remaining in the perfect will of God, you allow his supernatural power to continuously flow into your life, and obeying his Word keeps you connected to him.

NEWS ALERT

I know thy works, that thou art neither cold nor hot: I would thou wert cold or hot. So then because thou art lukewarm, and neither cold nor hot, I will spue thee out of my mouth (Revelation 3:15-16).

The title of a Christian requires us to live our lives conformed to the likeness of Christ. We are representing the almighty God and must be extremely cautious not to put him to shame. In this error, other than those seeking to establish or maintain a relationship with God, there aren't many folks reading their Bibles. Christians have taken the place of Bibles, and folks are now reading us. They're critiquing our behavior and comparing us to their beliefs of how a Christian should live and behave.

I personally believe that folks who proclaim to be Christians should conduct themselves in a Christ-like manner. You should conduct yourself in the same manner both in and out of the church. If you conduct yourself in a godly manner among believers, you should do the same among unbelievers. As believers, we represent the body of Christ; therefore, we should never conduct ourselves in a manner contrary to the Word of God.

Why should you attend regular church services if you are going to continue to live your life contrary to the Word of God (by fornicating, lying, backbiting, or committing adultery)? You can spare yourself the trouble of changing faces (being a hypocrite), because Jesus didn't hang on the cross from the sixth to the ninth hour for hypocrites. Jesus died for sinners, not pretenders!

When self-proclaimed Christians conduct themselves in a ungodly manner, their conduct hinders others from giving their lives to God. Think about it—if you witness someone who proclaims to be a Christian acting contrary to the Word of God, wouldn't his or her behavior affect your opinion of all Christians? I admit that if I were a sinner at a bar and I observed a pastor drinking alcohol, I would think, *He's no different than me.* In fact, I would probably think that there's no need to change my life, because chances are that I can make it into heaven just as I am.

I notice that most Christians who are living their lives contrary to God's Word tend to justify their sins by making excuses and changing the Word of God to support their lifestyles. They proclaim to be saved but continue to live the same lives as before they received salvation. They hang out at nightclubs and attend comedy shows where the comedian is blaspheming against the Holy Ghost, and these Christians have the audacity to laugh. They engage in the acts of fornication, adultery, homosexuality, etc. Yet they have the boldness to say, "I am a Christian." How does the love of God dwell within them?

Christians don't live double lives; we are sincere about our beliefs, and we don't compromise our Christianity. A Christian's sole purpose is to please God and execute his purposes. Christians look toward things of the future. We don't look backwards at our past wherein our lives were void of Jesus Christ. Christians make positive changes. Christians make a difference in the lives of others.

What shall we say then? Shall we continue in sin, that grace may abound? (Romans 6:1)

The words of Jon'-a-dab the son of Ra'-cheb, that he commanded his sons not to drink wine, are performed; for unto this day they drink none, but obey their father's commandment: not withstanding I have spoken unto you, rising early and speaking; but ye hearkened not unto me (Jeremiah 35:14).

Blessed is the man that walketh not in the counsel of the ungodly, nor standeth in the way of sinners, nor sitteth in the seat of the scornful (Psalm 1:1).

Submit yourselves therefore to God. Resist the devil, and he will flee from you. Draw nigh to God, and he will draw nigh to you. Cleanse your hands, ye sinners; and purify your hearts, ye double minded (James 4:7-8).

There is therefore now no condemnation to them which are in Christ Jesus, who walk not after the flesh, but after the Spirit . . . For they that are after the flesh do mind the things of the flesh; but they that are after the Spirit the things of the Spirit. For to be carnally minded is death; but to be spiritually minded is life and peace. Because the carnal mind is enmity against God: for it is not subject to the law of God, neither indeed can be. So then they that are in the flesh cannot please God (Romans 8:1, 5-8).

A double minded man is unstable in all his ways (James 1:8).

For as he thinketh in his heart, so is he: Eat and drink, saith he to thee; but his heart is not with thee (Proverbs 23:7).

Wherefore come out from among them, and be ye separate, saith the Lord, and touch not the unclean thing; and I will receive you (2 Corinthians 6:17).

Fools make a mock at sin: but among the righteous there is favour (Proverbs 14:9).

NO MORE EXCUSES!

As Christians, we must govern ourselves according to the Word of God. We can't have a part-time affair with a full-time God. In today's society, people are proclaiming Christianity but are living their lives contrary to the Word of God while making excuses for their sins. Our Christian beliefs should never be compromised, as God expects us to be faithful until the end.

But he that shall endure until the end, the same shall be saved (Matthew 24:13).

Hypocrites commit their bodies to fornication, alcoholism, drugs, lies, nightclubs, ungodly parties, strip clubs, etc. Then, following their actions, they begin to use some of the most common excuses, such as, "It was my last time." "We all have sinned; besides, no one is perfect." "I only went to support the cause." "God knows that we have sexual needs." "Show me in the Bible where it says Christians can't drink. Didn't Jesus turn water into wine?" These excuses—among many others—are used to justify sin. Sin grieves the Holy Spirit and can't be justified.

And grieve not the holy Spirit of God, whereby ye are sealed unto the day of redemption (Ephesians 4:30).

Would you like it if your children indulged in the things which you have forbidden them? Would you approve of your children walking in a disorderly way before the Lord?

For yourselves know how ye ought to follow us: for we behaved not ourselves disorderly among you (2 Thessalonians 3:7).

If you don't want your children to walk in a disorderly way, then you must lead by example, because your life affects the lives of others especially your children.

For none of us liveth to himself, and no man dieth to himself (Romans 14:7).

Once Jesus was crucified, there were no more excuses, as excuses were also crucified along with him. When you knowingly neglect the Word of God, the act is recognized as willful sin. Sin is harmful to you and others and is the doorway for the enemy to gain entry into your life.

For if we sin wilfuly after that we have received the knowledge of the truth, there remaineth no more sacrifice for sins, But a certain fearful looking for of judgment and fiery indignation, which shall devour the adversaries (Hebrews 10:26-27).

HOW CAN YOU WITNESS TO THE LOST IF YOU, TOO, ARE LOST?

Let them alone: they be blind leaders of the blind. And if the blind lead the blind, both shall fall into the ditch (Matthew 15:14).

HOW CAN YOU SERVE TWO MASTERS?

It is impossible to have a relationship with God and the enemy, too. Unfortunately, people proclaim that they are Christians, even though they divide their time between the enemy and God. In their hearts, they truly believe that it's acceptable to give God two days and the enemy five days a week of their time.

No man can serve two masters: for either he will hate the one, and love the other; or else he would hold to the one, and despise the other. Ye cannot serve God and mammon (Matthew 6:24).

God didn't come to place restrictions upon our pleasures but to maximize them.

The thief cometh not, but for to steal, and to kill, and to destroy: I am come that they might have life, and that they might have it more abundantly (John 10:10).

IDOLATRY

According to Webster's New Compact Dictionary an idol is an image made of a god, used as an object of worship, and/or any object or ardent or excessive devotion. Idolatry is worship of idols—excessive reverence for or devotion to a thing. To idolize something is to make an idol of or to love and/or admire someone excessively.

God forbids us from worshiping idols or having any affiliation with those things that threaten our relationship with him. Often, idols are mistakenly perceived to be molded images or anything in their likeness. However, this is a deadly deception that the enemy has used to mislead God's people.

An idol doesn't necessarily have to be a molded image, neither do you have to bow before it to be considered an idolatrous. Idolatry consists of anything or anyone who has taken the place of God in your life and can be your spouse, children, career, home, vehicle, money, drugs, alcohol, food, sex, etc. If you're guilty of allowing your relationship with God to be affected by your affiliation with someone or something, you must repent with a sincere heart. You must return unto your first love (God) and allow him to take his rightful place as first in your life.

Nevertheless I have somewhat against thee, because thou hast left thy first love (Revelation 2:4).

Mortify therefore your members which are upon the earth; fornication, uncleanness, inordinate affection, evil concupiscence, and covetousness, which is idolatry (Colossians 3:5).

Thou shalt have no other gods before me. Thou shalt not make unto thee any graven image, or any likeness of any thing that is in heaven above, or that is in the earth beneath, or that is in the water under the earth: Thou shalt not bow down thyself to them, nor serve them: for I the LORD thy God am a jealous God, visiting the iniquity of the fathers upon the children unto the third and fourth generation of them that hate me (Exodus 20:3-5).

Assemble yourselves and come; draw near together, ye that are escaped of the nations: they have no knowledge that set up the wood of their graven image, and pray unto a god that cannot save (Isaiah 45:20).

They bear him upon the shoulder, they carry him, and set him in his place, and he standeth; from his place shall he not remove: yea, one shall cry unto him, yet can he not answer, nor save him out of his trouble (Isaiah 46:7).

Among the smooth stones of the stream is thy portion; they, they are thy lot: even to them hast thou poured a drink offering, thou hast offered a meat offering. Should I receive comfort in these? (Isaiah 57:6)

A people that provoketh me to anger continually to my face; that sacrificeth in gardens, and burneth incense upon alters of brick (Isaiah 65:3).

And I will utter my judgments against them touching all their wickedness, who have forsaken me, and have burned incense unto other gods, and worshipped the works of their own hands (Jeremiah 1:16).

The children gather wood, and the fathers kindle the fire, and the women knead their dough, to make cakes to the queen of heaven, and to pour out drink offerings unto other gods, that they may provoke me to anger (Jeremiah 7:18).

Were they ashamed when they had committed abomination? Nay, they were not at all ashamed, neither could they blush: therefore shall they fall among them that fall: in the time of their visitation they shall be cast down, saith the LORD (Jeremiah 8:12).

They are vanity, and the work of errors: in the time of their visitation they shall perish (Jeremiah 10:15).

Then shall the cities of Judah and inhabitants of Jerusalem go, and cry unto the gods unto whom they offer incense: but they shall not save them at all in the time of their trouble (Jeremiah 11:12).

And they built the high places of Ba'-al, which are in the valley of the son of Hin'-nom, to cause their sons and their daughters to pass through the fire unto Mo'-lech; which I commanded them not, neither came it into my mind, that they should do this abomination, to cause Judah to sin (Jeremiah 32:35).

But we will certainly do whatsoever thing goeth forth out of our own mouth, to burn incense unto the queen of heaven, and to pour out drink offerings unto her, as we have done, we, and our fathers, our kings, and our princes, in the cities of Judah, and in the streets of Jerusalem: for then had we plenty of victuals, and were well, and saw no evil (Jeremiah 44:17).

I found Israel like grapes in the wilderness; I saw your fathers as the firstripe in the fig tree at her first time: but they went to Ba'-al-pe'-or, and separated themselves unto that shame; and their abominations were according as they loved (Hosea 9:10).

But I have a few things against thee, because thou hast there them that hold the doctrine of Ba'-laam, who taught Ba'-lac to cast a stumblingblock before the children of Israel, to eat things sacrificed unto idols, and to commit fornication (Revelation 2:14).

Neither be ye idolaters, as were some of them; as it is written, The people sat down to eat and drink, and rose up to play . . . Wherefore, my dearly beloved, flee from idolatry (1 Corinthians 10:7, 14).

Little children, keep yourselves from idols. A-men (1 John 5:21).

Their sorrows shall be multiplied that hasten after another god: their drink offerings of blood will I not offer, nor take up their names into my lips (Psalm 16:4).

Go and cry unto the gods which ye have chosen; let them deliver you in the time of your tribulation (Judges 10:14).

WHAT ARE EXCUSES?

According to *Webster's New Compact Dictionary,* excuses are made to justify, pardon, or release from an obligation. Sin cannot be justified, although through Jesus Christ, our sins can be pardoned; however, we are obligated to obey God's Word.

There are many people in the world who have knowledge of the truth but choose to sin anyhow. When one knowingly sins, it is recognized as willful sinning, for which there are consequences. When one sins, although he or she repents, there are still consequences that one has to endure. Again, there aren't any excuses for sin. Following are some biblical verses of excuses:

And the LORD God said unto the woman, What is this that thou hast done? And the woman said, The serpent beguiled me, and I did eat (Genesis 3:13).

Then the word of the LORD came unto me, saying, Before I formed thee in the belly I knew thee; and before thou camest forth out of the womb I sanctified thee, and I ordained thee a prophet unto the nations. Then said I, Ah, LORD GOD! Behold, I cannot speak: for I am a child. But the LORD said unto me, Say not, I am a child: for thou shalt go to all that I shall send thee, and whatsoever I command thee thou shalt speak (Jeremiah 1:4-7).

And Moses said unto the LORD, O my Lord, I am not eloquent, neither heretofore, nor since thou hast spoken unto thy servant: but I am slow of speech, and of a slow tongue. And the LORD said unto him, Who hath made man's mouth? Or who maketh the dumb, or deaf, or the seeing, or the blind? Have not I the LORD? Now therefore go, and I will be with thy mouth, and teach thee what thou shalt say. And he said, O my Lord, send, I pray thee, by the hand of him whom thou wilt send. And the anger of the LORD was kindled against Moses, and he said, Is not Aaron the Levite thy brother? I know that he can speak well. And also, behold, he cometh forth to meet thee: and when he seeth thee, he will be glad in his heart (Exodus 4:10-14).

For the invisible things of him from the creation of the world are clearly seen, being understood by the things that are made, even his eternal power and Godhead; so that they are without excuse (Romans 1:20).

Therefore thou art inexcusable, O man, whosoever thou art that judgest: for wherein thou judgest another, thou condemnest thyself; for thou that judgest doest the same things (Romans 2:1).

And another of his disciples said unto him, Lord, suffer me first to go and bury my father (Matthew 8:21).

And he said unto another, Follow me. But he said, Lord, suffer me first to go and bury my father. Jesus said unto him, Let the dead bury their dead: but go thou and preach the kingdom of God. And another also said, Lord, I will follow thee; but let me first go bid them farewell, which are at home at my house. And Jesus said unto him, No man, having put his hand to the plough, and looking back, is fit for the kingdom of God (Luke 9:59-62).

And they all with one consent begin to make excuse. The first said unto him, I have bought a piece of ground, and I must needs go and see it: I pray thee have me excused. And another said, I have bought five yoke of oxen, and I go to prove them: I pray thee have me excused. And another said, I have married a wife, and therefore I cannot come (Luke 14:18-20).

And Moses answered and said, But, behold, they will not believe me, nor hearken unto my voice: for they will say, The LORD hath not appeared unto thee (Exodus 4:1).

And he said, Who told thee that thou wast naked? Hast thou eaten of the tree, whereof I commanded thee that thou shouldest not eat? And the man said, The woman whom thou gavest to be with me, she gave me of the tree, and I did eat (Genesis 3:11-12).

THE POWER OF A WOMAN

Since the beginning of time, woman have possessed the power to influence man. In fact, many great men have fallen because of the negative influences of women. According to the Scriptures below, it is evident that the women in these verses utilized their powers in a negative manner.

In my opinion, if all wives were to learn to use their power in a positive way, as a result, their husbands would be pleased, and they probably would not seek pleasure in other women. I recall a quote from Bishop Austin Lawrence: "A poor frog doesn't praise his own pond." In effort to prevent living up to this quote, women should praise their husbands. For example, women must give their husbands love, care, sex, respect, encouragement, praise and show appreciation. In return, women will reap the benefits of a greater marriage. All women should practice utilizing the power of their influence positively.

And when the woman saw that the tree was good for food, and that it was pleasant to the eyes, and a tree to be desired to make one wise, she took of the fruit thereof, and did eat, and gave also unto her husband with her; and he did eat (Genesis 3:6).

And she said unto him, How canst thou say, I love thee, when thine heart is not with me? Thou hast mocked me these three times, and hast not told me wherein thy great strength lieth. And it came to pass, when she pressed him daily with her words, and urged him, so that his soul was vexed unto death; That he told her all his heart, and said unto her There hath not come a razor upon mine head; for I have been a Nazarite unto God from my mother's womb. If I be shaven, then my strength will go from me, and I shall become weak, and be like any other man.

And when De-li'-lah saw that he had told her all his heart, she sent and called for the lords of the Phi-lis'-tines, saying, Come up this once, for he hath shewed me all his heart. Then the lords of the Phi-lis'-tines came up unto her, and brought money in their hand. And she made him sleep upon her knees; and she called for a man, and she caused him to shave off the seven locks of his head; and she begin to afflict him, and his strength went from him. And she said, The Phi-lis'-tines be upon thee, Samson. And he awoke out of his sleep, and said, I will go out as other times before, and shake myself. And he wist not that the LORD was departed from him. But the Phi-lis'-tines took him, and put out his eyes, and brought him down to Ga'-za, and bound him with fetters of brass; and he did grind in the prison house (Judges 16:15-21).

For it came to pass, when Solomon was old, that his wives turned away his heart after other gods: and his heart was not perfect with the LORD his God, as was the heart of David his father (1 Kings 11:4).

And it came to pass, as if it had been a light thing for him to walk in the sins of Jer-o-bo'-am the son of Ne'-bat, that he took to wife Jez'-e-bel the daughter of Eth'-ba-al king of the Zi-do'-ni-ans, and went and served Ba'-al, and worshipped him. And he reared up an alter for Ba'-al in the house of Ba'-al, which he had built in Sa-ma'-ri-a. And Ahab made a grove; and Ahab did more to provoke the LORD God of Israel to anger than all the kings of Israel that were before him (1 Kings 16:31-33).

And it came to pass after these things, that his master's wife cast her eyes upon Joseph, and she said Lie with me. But he refused, and said un to his master's wife, Behold, my master wotteth not what is with me in the house, and he hath committed all that he hath to my hand; There is none greater in this house than I; neither hath he kept back any thing from me but thee, because thou art his wife: how then can I do this great wickedness, and sin against God? And it came to pass, as she spake to Joseph day by day, that he hearkened not unto her, to lie by her, or to be with her. And it came to pass about this time, that Joseph went into the house to do his business; and there was none of the men of the house there within. And she caught him by his garment, saying, Lie with me: and he left his garment in her hand, and fled, and got him out. And it came to pass, when she saw that he had left his garment in her hand, and was fled forth, That she called unto the men of her house, and spake unto them, saying, See, he hath brought in an Hebrew unto us to mock us; he came in unto me to lie with me, and I cried with a loud voice. And it came to pass, when he heard that I lifted up my voice and cried, that he left his garment with me, and fled, and got him out. And she laid up his garment by her, until his lord came home. And she spake unto him according to these words, saying, The Hebrew servant, which thou hast brought unto us, came in unto me to mock me: And it came to pass, as I lifted up my voice and cried, that he left his garment with me, and fled out. And it came to pass, when his master heard the words of his wife, which she spake unto him, saying, After this manner did thy servant to me; that his wrath was kindled. And Joseph's master took him, and put him into the prison, a place where the king's prisoners were bound: and he was there in the prison (Genesis 39:7-20).

THE POWER OF THE TONGUE

According to Webster's New Compact Dictionary, the tongue is the muscular organ attached to the floor of the mouth that is used in tasting, chewing, and speaking.

Even so the tongue is a little member, and boasteth great things. Behold, how great a matter a little fire kindleth! (James 3:5)

Although the tongue is the smallest among its members, it is very powerful and can be used as a deadly weapon to destroy the lives of others. The tongue has been the primary source of the destruction of countless relationships. However, believers must choose their words wisely in effort to restrain the tongue. One cannot represent God effectively if he or she doesn't have power to control his or her own words and is considered to be a fool.

For a dream cometh through the multitude of business; and a fool's voice is known by multitude of words (Ecclesiastes 5:3).

A fool also is full of words: a man cannot tell what shall be: and what shall be after him, who can tell him? (Ecclesiastes 10:14)

What does the Bible say about the tongue?

And the tongue is a fire, a world of iniquity: so is the tongue among our members, that it defileth the whole body, and setteth on fire the course of nature; and it is set on fire of hell (James 3:6).

If any man among you seem to be religious, and bridleth not his tongue, but deceiveth his own heart, this man's religion is vain (James 1:26).

I SAID, I will take heed to my ways, that I sin not with my tongue: I will keep my mouth with a bridle, while the wicked is before me (Psalm 39:1).

Death and life are in the power of the tongue: and they that love it shall eat the fruit thereof (Proverbs 18:21).

Whoso keepeth his mouth and his tongue keepeth his soul from troubles (Proverbs 21:23).

BRIDLE

According to Webster's New Compact Dictionary, a bridler is a leather harness used to place in a horse's mouth to control it. The Holy Ghost is what Christians rely upon for the power to bridle our tongues.

Behold, we put bits in the horses' mouths, that they may obey us; and we turn about their whole body (James 3:3).

Example: Sue has had a terrible day at work on today, and on her way home, she had a flat tire. Sue was exhausted but had to wait two hours for a tow truck to arrive. When the tower arrived, he was very rude toward Sue, but instead of being rude towards him, Sue smiled and said, "Thank you, sir; Jesus loves you."

Explanation: Sue could've used the excuse that she was having an awful day to curse, insult or yell at the tower but instead, she chose to bridle her tongue. In other words she chose to display kindness instead of rudeness. She bridled her tongue by holding her peace.

What does the Bible say about bridling the tongue?

For in many things we offend all. If any man offend not in word, the same is a perfect man, and able also to bridle the whole body . . . Behold also the ships, which though they be so great, and are driven of fierce winds, yet are they turned about with a very small helm, withersoever the governor listeth . . . For every kind of beasts, and of birds, and of serpents, and of things in the sea, is tamed, and hath been tamed of man kind. But the tongue can no man tame; it is an unruly evil, full of deadly poison. Therewith bless we God, even the Father; and therewith curse we men, which are made after the similitude of God. Out of the same mouth proceedeth blessing and cursing. My brethren, these things ought not so to be. Doth a fountain send forth at the same place sweet water and bitter? Can the fig tree, my brethren, bear olive berries? either a vine, figs? so can no fountain both yield salt water and fresh (James 3:2, 4, 7-12).

LIE, LIE, OH LIAR!

According to Webster's New Compact Dictionary, a lie is a false or untrue statement. A liar is a person who tells falsehoods.

But the fearful, and unbelieving, and the abominable, and murderers, and whoremongers, and sorcerers, and idolaters, and all liars, shall have their part in the lake which burneth with fire and brimstone: which is the second death (Revelation 21:8).

God represents the truth and is recognized as the only true God.

And this is life eternal, that they might know thee the only true God, and Jesus Christ, whom thou hast sent (John 17:3).

According to the Bible, we must worship God in spirit and in truth.

God is a Spirit: and they that worship him must worship him in spirit and in truth (John 4:24).

A liar is deceptive and has no place with God. A lie can be prevented, and a liar can stop deceiving others. Some people are misled into believing that there is such thing a as a white lie. However, whenever one knowingly gives a false statement, it is a lie, no matter what colors you choose to paint it!

Example: Christian is out having lunch at her favorite restaurant with a couple of her girlfriends. Her cellphone suddenly rings, and it is her husband, Marvin, who questions her whereabouts. Christian tells Marvin that she's still at work and he believes her.

Explanation: Instead of being honest concerning her whereabouts Christian chose to lie to intentionally deceive her husband.

Lie not one to another, seeing that ye have put off the old man with his deeds (Colossians 3:9).

What does the Bible say about a liar?

Behold, ye trust in lying words, that cannot profit. Will ye steal, murder, and commit adultery, and swear falsely, and burn incense unto Ba'-al, and walk after other gods whom ye know not (Jeremiah 7:8-9).

Ye are of your father the devil, and the lusts of your father ye will do. He was a murderer from the beginning, and abode not in the truth, because there is no truth in him. When he speaketh a lie, he speaketh of his own: for he is a liar, and the father of it (John 8:44).

A false witness shall not be unpunished, and he that speaketh lies shall shall perish (Proverbs 19:9).

A righteous man hateth lying: but a wicked man is loathsome, and cometh to shame (Proverbs 13:5).

A man that beareth false witness against his neighbour is a maul, and a sword, and a sharp arrow (Proverbs 25:18).

Add thou not unto his words, lest he reprove thee, and thou be found a liar (Proverbs 30:6).

And there shall in no wise enter into it any thing that defileth, neither whatsoever worketh abomination, or maketh a lie: but they which are written in the Lamb's book of life (Revelation 21:27).

GOSSIPER, SLANDERER, AND BUSYBODY

According to Webster's New Compact Dictionary gossip is often malicious talk. A gossiper spreads or engages in gossip. To be idle is to do nothing, be inactive, move lazily or slowly, run at a slow speed or out of gear, be unemployed, or be inactive. Slander is a false statement that deliberately does harm to another's reputation. A busybody is an inquisitive person who interferes with someone else's business.

Although gossips, slanderers, and busybodies, are all in the same family, each has a slightly different role. A gossiper is responsible for spreading gossip, a slanderer spreads damaging information, and a busybody is an investigator.

People who indulge in this behavior are usually idle and often have no better way of occupying their time wisely. Therefore, without anything constructive to do, they begin meddling in the affairs of others. They telephone person after person and go from home to home, spreading hurtful and damaging rumors. Often the rumors are spread without certainty of facts. Gossip has destroyed many lives, homes, and relationships. Be careful when speaking against others!

And withal they learn to be idle, wandering about from house to house; and not only idle, but tattlers also and busybodies, speaking things which they ought not (1 Timothy 5:13).

Example: Girl, do you know that yesterday, Regina came home on her lunch break and caught Mark and another woman in her bed, having sex? I mean, I don't want to be the bearer of bad news, but I'm just saying. Girl, you know he is wrong for that. In fact, he's been cheating on that girl since their wedding night. Girl, rumor has it that he spent the night with his baby mama on the night of their wedding—can you believe that? I don't feel sorry for either of them. She is so stupid! She should've gotten rid of that loser long ago!

Explanation: The speaker is clearly a busybody indulging in gossip and slander. Instead of praying for her brother and sister she has chosen to participate in the spread of rumors.

Wherefore laying aside all malice, and all guile, and hypocrisies, and envies, and all evil speakings (1 Peter 2:1).

If a couple is experiencing marital problems, both the husband and wife are probably emotional wrecks and are very low in spirit. Why would someone delight in kicking a man who is already down? If it were your marriage, wouldn't you expect others to be mindful of your feelings during your most difficult times?

And as you would that men should do to you, do ye also to them likewise (Luke 6:31).

Therefore thou art inexcusable, O man, whosoever thou art that judgest: for wherein thou judgest another, thou condemnest thyself; for thou that judgest doest the same things (Romans 2:1).

What does the Bible say about gossipers, slanderers, and busybodies?

He also that is slothful in his work is brother to him that is a great waster (Proverbs 18:9).

For we hear that there are some which walk among you disorderly, working not at all, but are busybodies (2 Thessalonians 3:11).

O Timothy, keep that which is committed to thy trust, avoiding profane and vain babblings, and oppositions of science falsely so called (1 Timothy 6:20).

But shun profane and vain babblings: for they will increase unto more ungodliness (2 Timothy 2:16).

And that ye study to be quiet, and to do your own business, and to work with your own hands, as we commanded you (1 Thessalonians 4:11).

PROFANITY

Although most people use profanity to express emotions, it is unacceptable behavior for Christians. Believers of God have restrictions that we must adhere to in order to be effective in the expansion of the gospel of Jesus Christ. God is holy, and we who serve him must be holy in deed and communication.

Because it is written, Be ye holy; for I am holy (1 Peter 1:16).

But now ye also put off all these; anger, wrath, malice, blasphemy, filthy communication out of your mouth (Colossians 3:8).

According to the Bible, we are not to be conformed unto this world.

And be not conformed to this world: but be ye transformed by the renewing of your mind, that ye may prove what is that good, and acceptable, and perfect, will of God (Romans 12:2).

Therefore, there should be a differentiation between a non-believer and a Christian by moral character.

Example: Bobby Wilson was aware that his friend Mark Jacobs was experiencing marital problems and suggested to Mark to meet his friend who was a minister for counseling. Mark agreed to meet Bobby, the minister and two guys at a restaurant for lunch. When Mark arrived at the restaurant Bobby and the guys were all drinking, telling dirty jokes, using profanity and laughing. Since none of the guys conducted themselves as a Christian Mark was unable to recognize which of them was the minister.

Explanation: True Christians will always conduct themselves as believers and should never be confused as a non-believer because of their behavior.

FOOD FOR THOUGHT:

Christians shouldn't have to inform anyone of their Christianity, because true Christians are recognized by their behavior.

Be not deceived: evil communications corrupt good manners (1 Corinthians 15:33).

What does the Bible say about profanity?

Let no corrupt communication proceed out of your mouth, but that which is good to the use of edifying, that it may minister grace unto the hearers (Ephesians 4:29).

But as he which hath called you is holy, so be ye holy in all manner of conversation (1 Peter 1:15).

Let him eschew evil, and do good; let him seek peace, and ensue it (1 Peter 3:11).

Seeing then that all these things shall be dissolved, what manner of persons ought ye to be in all holy conversation and godliness (2 Peter 3:11).

Only let your conversation be as it becometh the gospel of Christ: that whether I come and see you, or else be absent, I may hear of your affairs, that ye stand fast in one spirit, with one mind striving together for the faith of the gospel (Philippians 1:27).

Remember them which have the rule over you, who have spoken unto you the word of God: whose faith follow, considering the end of their conversation (Hebrews 13:7).

If any man speak, let him speak as the oracles of God; if any man minister, let him do it as of the ability which God giveth: that God in all things may be glorified through Jesus Christ, to whom be praise and dominion for ever and ever. A-men (1 Peter 4:11).

Thou hast proved mine heart; thou hast visited me in the night; thou hast tried me; and shalt find nothing; I am purposed that my mouth shall not transgress (Psalm 17:3).

The mouth of a righteous man is a well of life: but violence covereth the mouth of the wicked (Proverbs 10:11).

DEVOURING WORDS

There are many people living in the world today who are suffering with emotional abuse from their past. Unfortunately, most of them were damaged as children. As a result of the damages, they are unable to live constructive lives. Most of them find it extremely difficult to move forward with their lives because of the lies of the enemy which have convinced them to believe that they are nothing and will never amount to anything.

The enemy uses people to accomplish his mission to destroy the lives of others through gossip, slander, and backbiting. In fact, homes have been broken and marriages and other relationships have been destroyed because of the power of the tongue. Most of all, members of the body of Christ have been wounded by the power of words! Do you really want to be held liable for damaging the life of another person with your tongue?

Are there any consequences for speaking idle words?

But I say unto you, That every idle word that men shall speak, they shall give account thereof in the day of judgment (Matthew 12:36).

It is my desire that all women will take heed of this book and apply this information to their daily lives. Throughout the course of writing this book, it has been my prayer that this book will make positive changes in the lives of all its readers. I can only pray that this information will restore, reconcile, and resurrect any damaged relationships. We must maintain fruitful relationships in order to be effective in the kingdom of God.

Concerning marriages, women must fulfill their wifely duties even if they feel that their husbands aren't worthy. It is always assuring to know that you gave your very best in your marriage even if your marriage fails (God forbid). If that happens, you wouldn't have anything to feel guilty about and no regrets. In fact, you would have the comfort of knowing that after giving your all, it simply wasn't meant to be.

In conclusion, although this book contains information that could assist in ushering you into your divine destiny, neither it nor any other reading material should ever replace the Holy Bible. I pray that this book is a blessing to you and your loved ones. May the blessings of God overflow in your life.

Love always,

Schonshary Chiffon

Let us labor therefore to enter into that rest, lest any man fall after the same example of unbelief. (Hebrews 4:11)

Blessed are ye when ye hearken unto the voice of the almighty God!

And it shall come to pass, if thou shalt hearken diligently unto the voice of the LORD thy God, to observe and to do all his commandments, which I command thee this day, that the LORD thy God will set thee on high above all nations of the earth: And all these blessings shall come on thee, and overtake thee, if thou shalt hearken unto the voice of the LORD thy God. Blessed shalt thy be in the city, and blessed shalt thy be in the field. Blessed shall be the fruit of thy body, and the fruit of thy ground, and the fruit of thy cattle, the increase of thy kine, and the flocks of thy sheep. Blessed shall be thy basket and thy store. Blessed shalt thy be when thou comest in, and blessed shalt thou be when thou goest out. The LORD shall cause thine enemies that rise up against thee to be smitten before thy face: they shall come out against thee one way, and flee before thee seven ways. The LORD shall command the blessings upon thee in thy storehouses, and in all that thou settest thine hand unto; and he shall bless thee in the land which the LORD thy God giveth thee. The LORD shall establish thee an holy people unto himself, as he hath sworn unto thee, if thou shalt keep the commandments of the LORD thy God, and walk in his ways. And all people of the earth shall see that thou art called by the name of the LORD; and they shall be afraid of thee. And the LORD shall make thee plenteous in goods, in the fruit of thy body, and in the fruit of thy cattle, and in the fruit of thy ground, in the land which the LORD sware unto thy fathers to give thee. The LORD shall open unto thee his good treasure, the heaven to give the rain unto thy land in his season, and to bless all the work of thine hand: and thou shalt lend unto many nations, and thou shalt not borrow. And the LORD shall make thee the head, and not the tail; and thou shalt be above only, and thou shalt not be beneath; if that thou hearken unto the commandments of the LORD thy God, which I command thee this day, to observe and to do them: And thou shalt not go aside from any of the words which I command thee this day, to the right hand, or to the left, to go after other gods to serve them (Deuteronomy 28:1-14).

Sin is an act of disobedience that separates us from God, and disobedience opens the door for curses to enter into our lives. By reading the biblical passages below, you will discover that the curses of disobedience exceed the blessings of obedience by far.

But it shall come to pass, if thou wilt not hearken unto the voice of the LORD thy God, to observe to do all his commandments and his statues which I command thee this day; that all these curses shall come upon thee, and overtake thee: Cursed shalt thy be in the city, and cursed shalt thou be in the field. Cursed shall be thy basket and thy store. Cursed shall be the fruit of thy body, and the fruit of thy land, the increase of thy kine, and the flocks of thy sheep. Cursed shalt thou be when thou comest in, and cursed shalt thou be when thou goest out. The LORD shall send upon thee cursing, vexation, and rebuke, in all that thou settest thine hand unto for to do, until thou be destroyed, and until thou perish quickly; because of the wickedness of thy doings, whereby thou hast forsaken me. The LORD shall make the pestilence cleave unto thee, until he have consumed thee from off the land, whither thou goest to possess it. The LORD shall smite thee with a consumption, and with a fever, and with an inflammation, and with an extreme burning, and with the sword, and with blasting, and with mildew; and they shall pursue thee until thou perish. And thy heaven that is over thy head shall be brass, and the earth that is under thee shall be iron. The LORD shall make the rain of thy land powder and dust: from heaven shall it come down upon thee, until thou be destroyed. The LORD shall cause thee to be smitten before thine enemies: thou shalt go out one way against them, and flee seven ways before them: and shalt be removed into all the kingdoms of the earth. And thy carcase shall be meat unto all fowls of the air, and unto the beasts of the earth, and no man shall fray them away. The LORD will smite thee with the botch of Egypt, and with the emerods, and with the scab, and with the itch, whereof thou canst not be healed. The LORD shall smite thee with madness, and blindness, and astonishment of heart: And thou shalt grope at noonday, as the blind gropeth in darkness, and thou shalt not prosper in thy ways: and thou shalt be only oppressed and spoiled evermore, and no man shall save thee. Thou shalt betroth a wife, and another man shall lie with her: thou shalt build an house, and thou shalt not dwell therein: thou shalt plant a vineyard, and shalt not gather the grapes thereof. Thine ox shall be slain before thine eyes, and thou shalt not eat thereof: thine ass shall be violently taken away from before thy face, and shall not be restored to thee: thy sheep shall be given unto thine enemies, and thou shalt have none to rescue them. Thy sons and thy daughters shall be given unto another people, and thine eyes shall look, and fail with longing for them all the day long: and there shall be no might in thine hand. The fruit of thy land, and all thy labours, shall a nation which thou knowest not eat up; and thou shalt be only oppressed and crushed alway: So that thou shalt be mad for the sight of thine eyes which thou shalt see. The LORD shall smite thee in the knees, and in the legs, with a sore botch that cannot be healed, from the sole of thy foot unto the top of thy head. The LORD shall bring thee, and thy king which thou shalt set over thee, unto a nation which neither thou nor thy fathers have known; and there shalt thy serve other gods, wood and stone. And thou shalt become an astonishment, a proverb, and a byword, among all nations whither the LORD shall lead thee. Thou shalt carry much seed out into the field, and shalt gather but little in; for the locust shall consume it. Thou shalt plant vineyards, and dress them, but shalt neither drink of the wine, nor gather the grapes; for the worms shall eat them.

Thou shalt have olive trees throughout all thy coasts, but thou shalt not anoint thyself with the oil; for thine olive tree shall cast his fruit. Thou shalt beget sons and daughters, but thou shalt not enjoy them; for they shall go into captivity. All thy trees and fruit of thy land shall the locust consume. The stranger that is within thee shall get up above thee very high; and thou shalt come down very low. He shall lend to thee, and thou shalt not lend to him: he shall be the head, and thou shalt be the tail. Moreover all these curses shall come upon thee, and shall pursue thee, and overtake thee, till thou be destroyed; because thou hearkenedst not unto the voice of the LORD thy God, to keep his commandments and his statues which he commanded thee: And they shall be upon thee for a sign and for a wonder, and upon thy seed for ever. Because thou servedst not the LORD thy God with joyfulness, and with gladness of heart, for the abundance of all things. Therefore shalt thy serve thine enemies which the LORD shall send against thee, in hunger, and in thirst, and in nakedness, and in want of all things: and he shall put a yoke of iron upon thy neck, until he have destroyed thee. The LORD shall bring a nation against thee from far, from the end of the earth, as swift as the eagle flieth; a nation whose tongue thou shalt not understand; A nation of fierce countenance, which shall not regard the person of the old, nor shew favour to the young: And he shall eat the fruit of thy cattle, and the fruit of thy land, until thou be destroyed: which also shall not leave thee either corn, wine, or oil, or the increase of thy kine, or flocks of thy sheep, until he have destroyed thee. And he shall besiege thee in all thy gates, until thy high and fenced walls come down, wherein thou trustedst, throughout all thy land: and he shall besiege thee in all thy gates throughout all thy land, which the LORD thy God hath given thee. And thou shalt eat the fruit of thine own body, the flesh of thy sons and of thy daughters, which the LORD thy God hath given thee, in the siege, and in the straitness, wherewith thine enemies shall distress thee: So that the man is tender among you, and very delicate, his eye shall be evil toward his brother, and toward the wife of his bosom, and toward the remnant of his children which he shall leave: So that he will not give to any of them of the flesh of his children whom he shall eat: because he hath nothing left him in the siege, and in the straitness, wherewith thine enemies shall distress thee in all thy gates. The tender and delicate woman among you, which would not adventure to set the sole of her foot upon the ground for delicateness and tenderness, her eye shall be evil toward the husband of her bosom, and toward her son, and toward her daughter, And toward her young one that cometh out from between her feet, and toward her children which she shall bear: for she shall eat them for want of all things secretly in the siege and straitness, wherewith thine enemy shall distress thee in thy gates. If thou wilt not observe to do all the words of this law that are written in this book, that thou mayest fear this glorious and fearful name, THE LORD THY GOD; Then the LORD will make thy plagues wonderful, and the plagues of thy seed, even great plagues, and of long continuance, and sore sickness, and of long continuance. Moreover he will bring upon thee all the diseases of Egypt, which thou wast afraid of; and they shall cleave unto thee. Also every sickness, and every plague, which is not written in the book of this law, them will the LORD bring upon thee, until thou be destroyed. And ye shall be left few in number, whereas ye were as the stars of heaven for multitude; because thou wouldest not obey the voice of the LORD thy God. And it shall come to pass, that as the LORD rejoiced over you to do you good, and to multiply you; so the LORD will rejoice over you to destroy you, and to bring you to nought; and ye shall be plucked from off the land whither thou goest to possess it. And the LORD shall scatter thee among all people, from the one end of the earth even unto the other; and there thou shalt serve other gods, which neither thou nor thy fathers have known, even wood and stone. And among these nations shalt thou find no ease, neither shall the sole of thy foot have rest: but the LORD shall give thee there a trembling heart, and failing of eyes, and sorrow of mind. And thy life shall hang in doubt before thee; and thou shalt fear day and night, and shalt have none assurance of thy life: In the morning thou shalt say, Would God it were even! And at even thou shalt say, Would God it were morning! for the fear of thine heart wherewith thou shalt fear, and for the sight of thine eyes which thou shalt see. And the LORD shall bring thee into Egypt again with ships, by the way whereof I spake unto thee, Thou shalt see it no more again: and there ye shall be sold unto your enemies for bondmen and bondwomen, and no man shall buy you (Deuteronomy 28:15-68).

FOOD FOR THOUGHT

For the wages of sin is death; but the gift of God is eternal life through Jesus Christ our Lord (Romans 6:23).

The above passage isn't necessarily limited to a physical death; it can also refer to a decrease in health and finances as well as destruction upon relationships. The gift of God is given to those who love him and obey his Word. However, this passage doesn't imply that one will never experience a physical death but that there will be life in his or her circumstances. Following the physical death, the souls of those who obey God's Word will not experience destruction (hell), but will rest eternally with King Jesus!

THANKS

I thank the almighty God for granting me the opportunity to sow this reading material into his kingdom in which I pray that each reader will benefit and prosper from the contents inside. Lord, I truly appreciate all of the many *blessings* that you have bestowed upon my family and me. We have made it this far because of your *grace* and *mercy*.

I love you, Lord, and I pray that you continue to cover my family and me in your blood and protect us from the snares of the enemy. Please continue to keep us, because we cannot keep ourselves. I cannot thank you enough for your goodness toward me. Hallelujah!

To my spiritual parents: you have done so much for my family that I don't know where to begin. In 1999, when I met Bishop Austin and Elder Lorraine Lawrence, I never thought that the careless young lady I was would become the responsible woman I am today. I was incomplete, but through your ministry, I've been made whole. It is through your profound, dynamic teaching and your boldness to preach the truth that my life has changed tremendously since 1999. The effectiveness of your ministry is responsible for all that I am and all that I have. Therefore, I encourage you to continue to be steadfast and unmovable, always abiding in the Word of the Lord, for your labor isn't in vain! I love you both very much, and I thank you sincerely for everything that you have done.

The Holy Ghost Powerhouse Pentecostal Church of God
546 NW 16th Street
Florida City, Florida 33033

To my husband Keopatick Gordon Sr: first of all, I would like to say *thank you* for being supportive of my ideas since the beginning of our relationship. I love you, and I'm appreciative of everything you have done for our family. I'm thankful to God for blessing us with twelve years of marriage, and although it hasn't been easy, we remained in the struggle together. I *respect* you for your commitment to our wedding vows. I appreciate all of the marriage experiences (good and bad) we have had together, because those experiences inspired me to write this book. I love you unconditionally, and I pray that God gives us lots of years to enjoy our lives together. You are my "Boaz" and with God's help I will always love you!

To my mother: thank you for being the best mother that you possibly can be. I love you, and I appreciate all that you have sacrificed in an effort to provide a good upbringing for my siblings and me. I want you to know that those sacrifices weren't in vain. Therefore, on behalf of my siblings and myself, I commend you for a job well done. Again, I love you, and without a doubt, you are my *favorite* girl!

To my father: I would like to say that I forgave you long ago, and I encourage you to forgive yourself for any past mistakes. It is my belief that God never intended for us to hold on to a hurtful past, as our past has no relevance to our future. I appreciate you for being there when I needed you the most. You are a great father, and I wouldn't trade you for the world. I would never forget (through the Lord's help) when I was going through my trials that God used you to encourage, uplift, and inspire me with words of wisdom, and I will always love you for that. You are an *awesome* daddy; don't ever allow the enemy to tell you differently. I love you, Daddy!

To my uncle, Rev. A. E. Stewart: thank you for not being anything less than a father to my siblings and me; we love you dearly. You were always very genuine and kind; therefore, we were always certain that we could depend upon you, no matter how great our need. I thank you for choosing to focus on our needs rather than our flaws. Your acts of kindness toward us will never be forgotten, and on behalf of my siblings and me, we will *always* love you, Daddy!

To my uncles, Fred Stewart, Roger L. Stewart, and Morris Cannon: thanks for leading lives that inspired my siblings and me to be successful. We love you all dearly!

To my children, Brandy, Kiashani, Kiera, and Keopatrick, Jr.: I would like to thank each of you for believing in me. I love you all unconditionally. It is my desire for each of you girls to utilize this book as a reference guide to aid in maintaining fruitful relationships in the years to come. My son, I will save a copy for your future wife.

It is my prayer that God will cover each of you in his blood and direct your paths. I pray that he blesses each of you to succeed in your endeavors. I encourage you all to not just know of God, but also to build a personal relationship with him through prayer and worship. I love and desire the best for each of you. My children, you are my purpose. In fact, when you all came into my life, I stopped living my life for myself and began living my life for my children. Words could never express my feelings for you all, but just know that my love for my children will never die.

To my siblings, Vashika Gatewood, Gigi Harper, Atorrya Kennedy, Williesha Chaney, Trinicia Hewitt, Tiffany Bruce, Shanarrah Cannon, Cynthia Robbins, Winifred Gordon, and Marvin Cannon, Jr.: although each of you serves different purposes in my life, I love you all the same. I thank God for each of you and the unbreakable, inseparable bond that he has allowed us to have. I pray that things will *always* remain the same between us.

Like any family, we've experienced our share of differences, but at the end of the day, we love each other unconditionally. I can't thank any of you enough for being there to encourage me through all of my trials and tribulations. Also, thank you for listening to me go on and on about my book. I love each of you. You guys are the *best!*

Special thanks to my aunts, Falisha Bell and Ellen Stewart, for believing in me, being listening ears, and encouraging me.

Special thanks to Pastor Sherman Delva (Pastor Lucretia Delva) for believing in me and encouraging me to do the will of God.

Apostolic Faith and Deliverance
Center 660 W. Hillsboro Blvd
Deerfield Beach, Florida 33441
The Hampton Inn Hotel

Special thanks to my cousins, Dyrushio and Arashio Harris, for encouraging and uplifting me when I was low in spirit to continue to do the will of God

To my cousin, Dhafir Harris (aka DaDa 5000): may God continuously bestow his many blessings upon you. I love you!

To my co-worker and dear friend Herrick Derys, Thank you for believing in my vision, I love you and may God continuously bless you and your family!

Thanks to my Photographer Curtis Ballard for working diligently with me. I really appreciate all of your efforts to make my photos beautiful!

Thanks to my fashion designer Melvin Alexander for being one of the best designers in the world!

To my friend, hairstylist and make-up artist Delmar Lockhart, Thank you for all of the years of excellent service that you have rendered to me, and for always being there whenever I needed you. I love you!

To my dear friend and Esthetician Yvette Robinson Roberts, Thank you for all the years you have dedicated to providing me with excellent skin care services. I love you my dear sister and you are truly the best!

Yvette Robinson Roberts
Paramedical Esthetician/Electrolysis Laser Tech
Specializing in Acne Treatment
Microdermabrasion/Peels/Anti-aging Treatment

To my wonderful nephews and nieces who I love very dearly: Vincent Smith Jr and Dakevian (Kiki) Smith, Derrick Jackson Jr, Anthony (Payne) Charlton Jr, Dameko Labon, Damarcus (Big boy) Kennedy, Randy (Bam Bam) Charlton, Marvin (Mj) Burroughs Jr, James (Bloop) Gatewood Jr, Jontavis Testa, Jonathan Testa Jr, George (Petey) Knowles, Garret Knowles, Janiesha Troutman, Nataja Mair, Kevina Benjamin, Lavonda Gordon, Jazarah Alani Testa, Jada Star Harper and Makyah Kennedy. My love for you guys is unconditional, and it is my prayer that each of you will prosper and have great lives in the Lord. Therefore, I encourage each of you to seek the Lord in all things and allow him to be your guide.

To my brothers-in-law: James Lamount Gatewood Sr, Demetrius Harper and Marcus Kennedy and Donald Chaney Sr: I would like to take this opportunity to thank each of you for being "Boaz" to my sisters. You guys are the men that the Holy bible speaks of in terms of making provision for your families, and although I realize that you all aren't seeking any praises for conducting your God-given duties you are worthy of honor! Therefore, I commend each of you on a job well done! I encourage each of you to keep up the good work.

Thanks to Lee at Tip Nails for doing such a great job with my eyebrows and eyelashes. You're the best!

Tip Nails
18901 S. Dixie Hwy # 185-189
Miami, Florida 33157

Thanks to the crew at Nail Trap #7 for doing such a wonderful job with my manicures and pedicures. You guys are an awesome team!

Nail Trap No.7
18635 S. Dixie Hwy
Miami, Florida 33157

Special thanks to my dear sister Lillian James for all of your love and support. I truly love and appreciate you for being a friend that I can count on. May God continuously bless you forever!

To my cousins Jeffrey, Shaska and Rhian, I love you guys and may God continuously bless each of you.

To my god-sisters Ziphia, Xania and Yakitha, and god-brother Wykeem Lawrence: I love you guys and may God continuously bless each of you in all of your endeavors!

To my Powerhouse family, I love you all and may God bless each of you abundantly.

Latrovious Durham, Misty Reeves, Lisa Williams, Nicole Martinez and Markedia Horn, Smile, Jesus truly loves each of you and so do I! ;0)

To my wonderful friend Steven Bridges, I appreciate you for being a genuine friend over the years, I love you

To my dear friend Stanley Marcel, since the first day of our friendship you haven't be anything less than a true friend to me, and for that I genuinely love you.

To Hezekiah President, Samuel Josue, Lisa Eutsey, and Warren Hodge: May God bless & forever keep you guys.

If I have failed to mention any names please forgive me, and know that even if you aren't always in my head you are forever in my heart...

Made in United States
Orlando, FL
15 January 2022

13485244R00104